중학 영작문

내공

중학
영작문 **1**

저자 약력

전지원

미국 오리건 주립대 석사
한국 외국어대학교 외국어연수 평가원 영어 전임강사(현)

〈Grammar's Cool〉(YBM), 〈빠르게 잡는 영문법〉(천재교육),
〈Grammar plus Writing〉(다락원), 〈Grammar plus Writing Start〉(다락원),
〈It's NEAT Speaking Basic / Listening Basic〉(에듀조선) 등 다수의 교재 공저

박혜영

미국 하와이 주립대 석사
한국 외국어대학교 외국어연수 평가원 영어 전임강사(현)

〈Grammar's Cool〉(YBM), 〈빠르게 잡는 영문법〉(천재교육),
〈Grammar plus Writing〉(다락원), 〈Grammar plus Writing Start〉(다락원),
〈It's NEAT Speaking Basic / Listening Basic〉(에듀조선) 등 다수의 교재 공저

내공 중학 영작문 ①

지은이 전지원, 박혜영
펴낸이 정규도
펴낸곳 (주)다락원

초판 1쇄 발행 2017년 12월 18일
초판 8쇄 발행 2023년 12월 27일

편집 서정아, 김미경
디자인 박나래
삽화 JUNO
영문 감수 Michael A. Putlack

다락원 경기도 파주시 문발로 211
내용문의 (02)736-2031 내선 503
구입문의 (02)736-2031 내선 250~252
Fax (02)732-2037
출판등록 1977년 9월 16일 제 406-2008-000007호

ISBN 978-89-277-0814-8 54740
     978-89-277-0813-1 54740 (set)

http://www.darakwon.co.kr
다락원 홈페이지를 방문하시면 상세한 출판정보와 함께
동영상강좌, MP3자료 등 다양한 어학 정보를 얻으실 수 있습니다.

중학 영작 + 서술형 대비

내공 중학 영작문 1

전지원, 박혜영

DARAKWON

HOW TO STUDY THIS BOOK

STEP 1   LEARN

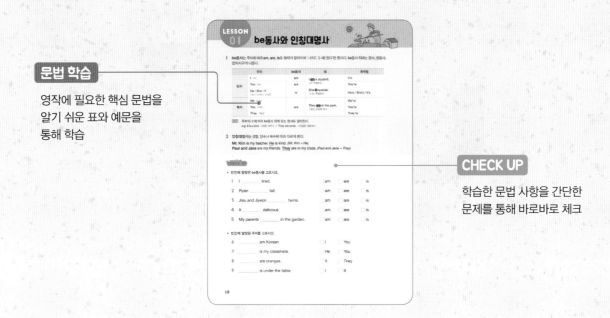

문법 학습

영작에 필요한 핵심 문법을
알기 쉬운 표와 예문을
통해 학습

CHECK UP

학습한 문법 사항을 간단한
문제를 통해 바로바로 체크

STEP 2   PRACTICE

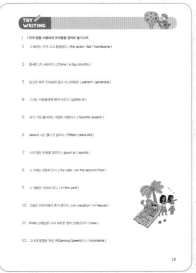

SENTENCE PRACTICE 1

학습한 문법을 포인트별로 하나씩
문장에 적용해보는 기초 연습

SENTENCE PRACTICE 2

학습한 문법을 포인트별로 다양한
문장에 적용해보는 연습

TRY WRITING

학습한 문법을 이용해 최종적으로
완전한 문장을 써보는 연습

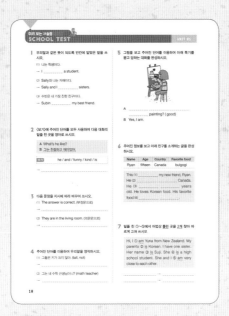

미리 보는 서술형 SCHOOL TEST

학교 시험에 대비할 수 있도록 실제 기출
문제를 응용한 서술형 문제로 단원 마무리

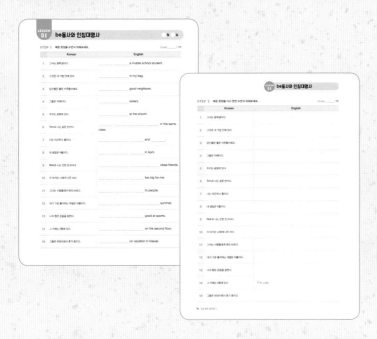

문장 암기 WORKBOOK

각 Lesson의 핵심 문장을 쓰고
읽으면서 암기할 수 있는
Workbook 제공

CONTENTS

UNIT
01

be동사

be동사와 인칭대명사

1 be동사는 주어에 따라 **am, are, is**로 형태가 달라지며 '~이다', '(~에) 있다'란 뜻이다. be동사 뒤에는 명사, 형용사, 전치사구가 나온다.

주어		be동사	예	축약형
단수	I 나는	am	I am a student. 나는 학생이다.	I'm
	You 너는	are		You're
	He / She / It 그는 / 그녀는 / 그것은	is	She is special. 그녀는 특별하다.	He's / She's / It's
복수	We 우리는	are	They are in the park. 그들은 공원에 있다.	We're
	You 너희는			You're
	They 그들은			They're

PLUS 주어의 수에 따라 be동사 뒤에 오는 명사도 달라진다.
e.g. It is *a bird*. 그것은 새이다. / They are *birds*. 그것들은 새들이다.

2 인칭대명사는 성별, 단수나 복수에 따라 다르게 쓴다.

Mr. Kim is my teacher. **He** is kind. *(Mr. Kim = He)*
Paul and Jane are my friends. **They** are in my class. *(Paul and Jane = They)*

CHECK UP

● 빈칸에 알맞은 be동사를 고르시오.

1 I _____ tired. ☐ am ☐ are ☐ is

2 Ryan _____ tall. ☐ am ☐ are ☐ is

3 Jisu and Jiyeon _____ twins. ☐ am ☐ are ☐ is

4 It _____ delicious. ☐ am ☐ are ☐ is

5 My parents _____ in the garden. ☐ am ☐ are ☐ is

● 빈칸에 알맞은 주어를 고르시오.

6 _____ am Korean. ☐ I ☐ You

7 _____ is my classmate. ☐ He ☐ You

8 _____ are oranges. ☐ It ☐ They

9 _____ is under the table. ☐ I ☐ It

box 안의 예문을 참고하여 우리말과 일치하도록 문장을 완성하시오.

WRITING POINT ❶

- I **am** hungry. 나는 / 이다 / 배고픈 (배고프다)
- You **are** at home. 너는 / 있다 / 집에
- He **is** my English teacher. 그는 / 이다 / 나의 영어 선생님

---

1 나는 힘이 세다.   I _____ strong.

2 너는 노래를 잘한다.   You _____ a good singer.

3 그는 나의 사촌이다.   He _____ my cousin.

4 그녀는 중학생이다.   She _____ a middle school student.

5 그것은 내 가방 안에 있다.   It _____ in my bag.

6 그 강아지는 귀엽다.   The puppy _____ cute.

7 이 공책은 내 것이다.   This notebook _____ mine.

8 James 선생님은 교실에 계신다.   Mr. James _____ in the classroom.

WRITING POINT ❷

- They **are** my grandparents. 그들은 / 이다 / 나의 조부모님

---

1 너희는 나의 친구들이야.   You _____ my friends.

2 당신들은 좋은 이웃들이에요.   You _____ good neighbors.

3 그들은 자매이다.   They _____ sisters.

4 그들은 축구 선수들이다.   They _____ soccer players.

5 우리는 공항에 있다.   We _____ at the airport.

6 그 게임들은 재미있다.   Those games _____ fun.

7 Philip과 Sue는 수학을 잘한다.   Philip and Sue _____ good at math.

8 Tom과 나는 같은 반이다.   Tom and I _____ in the same class.

우리말과 일치하도록 빈칸에 알맞은 말을 넣으시오.

• 단수 주어 + be동사 •

1 나는 피곤하고 졸리다. (tired / sleepy)

→ _____ _____ _____ and _____.

2 감사합니다. 당신은 참 친절하군요. (kind)

→ Thank you. _____ _____ so _____.

3 그녀의 이름은 Jessica이다. (name)

→ _____ _____ _____ Jessica.

4 그 남자는 호주 출신이다. (the man)

→ _____ _____ _____ from Australia.

5 내 생일은 4월이다. (birthday)

→ _____ _____ _____ in April.

• 복수 주어 + be동사 •

6 그들은 일하느라 바쁘다. (busy)

→ _____ _____ _____ with their work.

7 Rick과 나는 친한 친구이다.

→ _____ _____ _____ _____ close friends.

8 너희는 여전히 젊고 아름다워. (young / beautiful)

→ _____ _____ still _____ and _____.

9 그 아이들은 수영장에 있다. (the children)

→ _____ _____ _____ in the swimming pool.

10 이 바지는 나에게 너무 크다. (these pants / too big)

→ _____ _____ _____ _____ _____ for me.

( ) 안의 말을 이용하여 우리말을 영어로 옮기시오.

1 그 배우는 키가 크고 잘생겼다. (the actor / tall / handsome)

2 중국은 큰 나라이다. (China / a big country)

3 당신은 매우 인내심이 많고 너그러워요. (patient / generous)

4 그녀는 사람들에게 예의 바르다. (polite to)

5 내가 가장 좋아하는 계절은 여름이다. (favorite season)

6 Jane과 나는 열다섯 살이다. (fifteen years old)

7 나의 형은 운동을 잘한다. (good at / sports)

8 그 카페는 2층에 있다. (the café / on the second floor)

9 그 개들은 마당에 있다. (in the yard)

10 그들은 하와이에서 휴가 중이다. (on vacation / in Hawaii)

11 Endly 선생님은 나의 새로운 영어 선생님이다. (new)

12 그녀의 별명은 댄싱 퀸(Dancing Queen)이다. (nickname)

LESSON
02
be동사의 부정문, 의문문

1 be동사의 부정문은 「be동사 + not」의 형태로 쓰며, '~이 아니다', '(~에) 없다'란 뜻이다.

주어	be동사 + not	예	축약형
I	am not	I am not a teacher. 나는 선생님이 아니다.	I'm not
He / She / It	is not		He/She/It isn't He's/She's/It's not
We / You / They	are not	They are not at home. 그들은 집에 없다.	We/You/They aren't We're/You're/They're not

2 be동사의 의문문은 「Be동사 + 주어 ~?」의 형태로 쓴다.

Be동사 + 주어 ~?	예
Am I ~?	Is she a doctor? 그녀는 의사니?
Is he/she/it ~?	
Are we/you/they ~?	Are they expensive? 그것들은 비쌉니까?

NOTE be동사 의문문에 대한 답은 「Yes, 주어 + am/are/is.」, 「No, 주어 + 'm not/isn't/aren't.」로 한다.
e.g. Is Minho your brother? – *Yes*, he *is*. / *No*, he *isn't*.
Are you hungry? – *Yes*, I *am*. / *No*, I'm *not*.

CHECK UP

● 빈칸에 알맞은 말을 고르시오.

1 I _____ thirsty now.　　☐ am not　☐ are not

2 _____ you a good swimmer?　　☐ Am　☐ Are

3 We _____ late for class.　　☐ is not　☐ are not

4 _____ he from Japan?　　☐ Is　☐ Are

5 Sumi and I _____ very close.　　☐ am not　☐ are not

● 밑줄 친 부분의 줄임말을 쓰시오.

6 I <u>am not</u> hungry.　　_____

7 It <u>is not</u> a good idea.　　_____

8 He <u>is not</u> in the office.　　_____

9 They <u>are not</u> my toys.　　_____

box 안의 예문을 참고하여 우리말과 일치하도록 문장을 완성하시오.

> **WRITING POINT ①**
>
> • I **am not** tired. 나는 / 아니다 / 피곤한 (피곤하지 않다)
> • It **is not** our dog. 그것은 / 아니다 / 우리 개가
> • They **are not** at school. 그들은 / 없다 / 학교에

I 나는 요리를 잘 못해.

I _____ _____ a good cook.

2 너는 게으르지 않다.

You _____ _____ lazy.

3 그는 나의 형이 아니다.

He _____ _____ my brother.

4 그녀는 그녀 방에 없다.

She _____ _____ in her room.

5 우리는 아직 준비되지 않았다.

We _____ _____ ready yet.

6 이 수프는 따뜻하지 않다.

This soup _____ _____ warm.

7 저 신발은 내 것이 아니다.

Those shoes _____ _____ mine.

> **WRITING POINT ②**
>
> • **Am I** wrong? 이니 / 나는 / 틀린 (틀렸니?)
> • **Is he** a famous writer? 이니 / 그는 / 유명한 작가?
> • **Are they** in class? 이니 / 그들은 / 수업 중?

I 너는 오늘 바쁘니?

_____ _____ busy today?

2 그는 오늘 한가하니?

_____ _____ free today?

3 내가 너의 가장 친한 친구니?

_____ _____ your best friend?

4 그것은 1층에 있나요?

_____ _____ on the first floor?

5 그들은 거실에 있나요?

_____ _____ in the living room?

6 Helen은 변호사입니까?

_____ Helen a lawyer?

7 Alex와 당신은 동갑입니까?

_____ Alex and you the same age?

8 그 책은 재미있니?

_____ the book interesting?

우리말과 일치하도록 빈칸에 알맞은 말을 넣으시오.

• be동사의 부정문 •

1   나는 거짓말쟁이가 아니야. (a liar)

→ I _____ _____ _____ _____ .

2   오늘은 날씨가 춥지 않다. (the weather / cold)

→ _____ _____ _____ _____ _____ today.

3   걱정 마. 너는 혼자가 아니야. (alone)

→ Don't worry. You _____ _____ _____ .

4   네 공책들은 책상 위에 없다. (notebooks)

→ _____ _____ _____ _____ on the desk.

5   그 상점은 일요일에 문을 열지 않는다. (the shop / open)

→ _____ _____ _____ _____ _____ on Sunday.

• be동사의 의문문 •

6   너는 음악에 관심이 있니? (interested in)

→ _____ _____ _____ _____ music?

7   너희 부모님은 엄격하시니? (parents)

→ _____ _____ _____ strict?

8   민호(Minho)는 나에게 화났니? (angry)

→ _____ _____ _____ with me?

9   우리 갈 준비 되었어요? (ready)

→ _____ _____ _____ to go?

10   John은 아직도 침대에 있니? (in bed)

→ _____ _____ still _____ _____ ?

( ) 안의 말을 이용하여 우리말을 영어로 옮기시오.

1 이 채소들은 신선하지 않다. (these vegetables / fresh)

2 이것은 네 가방이니? (this)

3 이번 주 토요일에 시간 있어요? (free / this Saturday)

4 그것은 내 휴대전화가 아니다. (it / cell phone)

5 그 영화는 재미있니? (the movie / interesting)

6 우리는 지금 수업 중이 아니다. (in class / right now)

7 미나(Mina)와 민지(Minji)는 쌍둥이니? (twins)

8 Brown 씨는 결혼하지 않았다. (married)

9 Pam과 Rachel은 같은 반이 아니다. (in the same class)

10 파란색이 네가 가장 좋아하는 색이니? (favorite color)

11 나는 스포츠에 관심이 없다. (interested in / sports)

12 당신은 개들을 무서워하나요? (afraid of / dogs)

1 우리말과 같은 뜻이 되도록 빈칸에 알맞은 말을 쓰시오.

(1) 나는 학생이다.

→ I _____ a student.

(2) Sally와 나는 자매이다.

→ Sally and I _____ sisters.

(3) 수빈은 내 가장 친한 친구이다.

→ Subin _____ my best friend.

2 〈보기〉에 주어진 단어를 모두 사용하여 다음 대화의 밑줄 친 곳을 영어로 쓰시오.

A What's he like?
B 그는 친절하고 재미있어.

보기   he / and / funny / kind / is

→ _____

3 다음 문장을 지시에 따라 바꾸어 쓰시오.

(1) The answer is correct. (부정문으로)

→ _____

(2) They are in the living room. (의문문으로)

→ _____

4 주어진 단어를 이용하여 우리말을 영작하시오.

(1) 그들은 키가 크지 않아. (tall, not)

→ _____

(2) 그는 네 수학 선생님이니? (math teacher)

→ _____

5 그림을 보고 주어진 단어를 이용하여 아래 특기를 묻고 답하는 대화를 완성하시오.

A _____ _____ _____
_____ painting? (good)
B Yes, I am.

6 주어진 정보를 보고 아래 친구를 소개하는 글을 완성하시오.

Name	Age	Country	Favorite food
Ryan	fifteen	Canada	bulgogi

This (1) _____ my new friend, Ryan.
He (2) _____ _____ Canada.
He (3) _____ _____ years
old. He loves Korean food. His favorite
food (4) _____ _____.

7 밑줄 친 ①~⑤에서 어법상 틀린 곳을 2개 찾아 바르게 고쳐 쓰시오.

Hi, I ① am Yuna from New Zealand. My
parents ② is Korean. I have one sister.
Her name ③ is Suji. She ④ is a high
school student. She and I ⑤ am very
close to each other.

_____ → _____

_____ → _____

UNIT
02

일반동사

I 일반동사는 eat(먹다), go(가다)처럼 동작이나 have(가지고 있다), like(좋아하다)처럼 상태를 나타내는 동사를 가리킨다. 일반동사는 주어가 he, she, it과 같은 3인칭 단수일 때 동사에 -(e)s를 붙인다.

주어	일반동사	예
I / You / We / They / 복수명사	동사원형	I go to school at 8 o'clock. 나는 8시에 학교에 간다. They play soccer on Sundays. 그들은 일요일마다 축구를 한다. Monkeys like bananas. 원숭이들은 바나나를 좋아한다.
He / She / It / 3인칭 단수	동사원형 + (e)s	He goes to bed early. 그는 일찍 잠자리에 든다. It rains a lot in summer. 여름에는 비가 많이 온다. My father works at a bank. 나의 아버지는 은행에서 일하신다.

2 일반동사 3인칭 단수형의 형태

대부분의 동사	+ s	eats, works, sleeps, meets, learns
-o, -s, -ch, -sh, -x로 끝나는 동사	+ es	goes, does, misses, teaches, washes, fixes
「자음 + y」로 끝나는 동사	y → i + es	studies, cries, flies, tries
「모음 + y」로 끝나는 동사	+ s	buys, plays, enjoys

NOTE have는 불규칙 동사로 주어가 3인칭 단수일 때 has를 쓴다.
e.g. She *has* a puppy. 그녀는 강아지 한 마리를 가지고 있다.

CHECK UP

● 빈칸에 알맞은 동사의 형태를 고르시오.

1 We _____ badminton every Saturday.　☐ play　☐ plays

2 She _____ up early in the morning.　☐ get　☐ gets

3 I usually _____ food at this store.　☐ buy　☐ buys

4 The baby _____ every night.　☐ cry　☐ cries

5 He _____ his homework after school.　☐ do　☐ does

6 It _____ a lot in Russia.　☐ snow　☐ snows

7 Joe and I _____ to the same school.　☐ go　☐ goes

8 The girl _____ beautiful eyes.　☐ have　☐ has

9 Water _____ at 0°C.　☐ freeze　☐ freezes

box 안의 예문을 참고하여 우리말과 일치하도록 문장을 완성하시오.

WRITING POINT ①

· I **go** to the gym every day. 나는 / 간다 / 체육관에 / 매일

---

1 나는 매일 아침을 먹는다.　　　　　　　I _____ breakfast every day.

2 너는 멋진 차를 가지고 있다.　　　　　　You _____ a nice car.

3 우리는 보통 학교에 걸어간다.　　　　　We usually _____ to school.

4 그들은 저녁에 TV를 본다.　　　　　　　They _____ TV in the evening.

5 그 학생들은 교복을 입는다.　　　　　　The students _____ school uniforms.

6 그의 부모님은 캐나다에 산다.　　　　　His parents _____ in Canada.

7 그 소녀들은 테니스를 매우 잘 친다.　　The girls _____ tennis very well.

8 Tom과 Sally는 아이스크림을 좋아한다.　Tom and Sally _____ ice cream.

9 그 과학자들은 로봇을 만든다.　　　　　The scientists _____ robots.

WRITING POINT ②

· She **practices** the violin every day. 그녀는 / 연습한다 / 바이올린을 / 매일

---

1 그는 저 집에 산다.　　　　　　　　　　He _____ in that house.

2 그는 버스로 학교에 간다.　　　　　　　He _____ to school by bus.

3 그녀는 의학을 공부한다.　　　　　　　She _____ medicine.

4 그녀는 학교에서 영어를 가르친다.　　　She _____ English at school.

5 Mike는 태국 음식을 즐긴다.　　　　　　Mike _____ Thai food.

6 내 여동생은 곱슬머리를 가지고 있다.　　My sister _____ curly hair.

7 그 영화는 10시에 시작한다.　　　　　　The movie _____ at 10.

8 그 말은 매우 빨리 달린다.　　　　　　　The horse _____ very fast.

9 Ann은 매년 크리스마스에 케이크를 산다.　Ann _____ a cake every Christmas.

우리말과 일치하도록 빈칸에 알맞은 말을 넣으시오.

• 1·2인칭/3인칭 복수 + 일반동사 •

I 나는 여름마다 제주도에 간다. (Jeju Island)

→ _____ _____ _____ _____ _____ every summer.

2 우리는 주말마다 야외 스포츠를 즐긴다. (outdoor sports)

→ _____ _____ _____ _____ on weekends.

3 너는 항상 나를 잘 이해해준다. (understand)

→ _____ _____ _____ well all the time.

4 Greg와 Kelly는 방과 후 도서관에서 공부한다.

→ _____ _____ _____ _____ in the library after school.

5 요즘에는 많은 외국인들이 한국어를 배운다. (many / foreigners / Korean)

→ _____ _____ _____ _____ these days.

• 3인칭 단수 + 일반동사 •

6 그는 보통 점심으로 샌드위치를 먹는다. (sandwiches)

→ _____ usually _____ _____ for lunch.

7 그 배우는 3개 국어를 말한다. (the actor)

→ _____ _____ _____ three languages.

8 민수(Minsu)는 여가 시간에 만화책을 읽는다. (comic books)

→ _____ _____ _____ _____ in his free time.

9 그녀는 수영장이 있는 멋진 집을 가지고 있다. (a nice house)

→ _____ _____ _____ _____ with a pool.

10 그의 개는 항상 나를 보고 짖는다. (bark)

→ _____ _____ always _____ at me.

( ) 안의 말을 이용하여 우리말을 영어로 옮기시오.

1 나는 아침에 늦게 일어난다. (get up / in the morning)

2 지호(Jiho)는 저녁 식사 후 컴퓨터 게임을 한다. (computer games / after dinner)

3 Cathy는 매일 아침 머리를 감는다. (wash her hair)

4 나의 할머니는 정원에서 토마토를 재배한다. (tomatoes / in her garden)

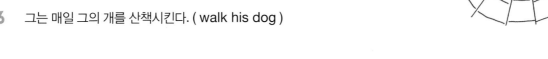

5 거미들은 다리가 8개이다. (spiders)

6 그는 매일 그의 개를 산책시킨다. (walk his dog)

7 Jones 씨 부부에게는 세 명의 자녀가 있다. (Mr. and Mrs. Jones / children)

8 우리는 매일 집을 청소한다. (the house)

9 많은 사람들이 그 공원에서 자전거를 탄다. (many / ride bicycles / in the park)

10 나의 형은 다른 나라들의 동전들을 수집한다. (coins from other countries)

11 그 새들은 매우 높이 난다. (high)

12 이 컴퓨터는 수리가 필요하다. (need / fixing)

일반동사의 부정문, 의문문

1 일반동사의 부정문은 주어에 따라 「**do/does not＋동사원형**」의 형태로 쓴다. do not과 does not은 각각 **don't**, **doesn't**로 줄여 쓸 수 있다.

I / You / We / They / 복수명사	He / She / It / 3인칭 단수
I like action movies.	He watches that TV show.
→ I do not[don't] like action movies.	→ He does not[doesn't] watch that TV show.
나는 액션 영화들을 좋아하지 않는다.	그는 그 TV 프로그램을 보지 않는다.

2 일반동사의 의문문은 주어에 따라 「**Do/Does＋주어＋동사원형 ~?**」의 형태로 쓴다.

I / You / We / They / 복수명사	He / She / It / 3인칭 단수
You enjoy Korean food.	She speaks English.
→ Do you enjoy Korean food?	→ Does she speak English?
당신은 한국 음식을 즐기나요?	그녀는 영어를 하나요?

NOTE 일반동사 의문문에 대한 답은 「Yes, 주어＋do/does.」, 「No, 주어＋don't/doesn't.」로 한다.
e.g. Do you have a pet? – *Yes*, I *do*. / *No*, I *don't*.
Does your father drive to work? – *Yes*, he *does*. / *No*, he *doesn't*.

CHECK UP

● 빈칸에 알맞은 말을 고르시오

I   I _____ get up early in the morning. ☐ don't ☐ doesn't

2   _____ you want more sauce? ☐ Do ☐ Does

3   She _____ care about other people. ☐ don't ☐ doesn't

4   _____ they often go to the movies? ☐ Do ☐ Does

5   They _____ like each other. ☐ don't ☐ doesn't

6   Sarah _____ know about the country. ☐ don't ☐ doesn't

7   Some people _____ eat meat or fish. ☐ don't ☐ doesn't

8   _____ Sam and Sally know each other? ☐ Do ☐ Does

9   My father _____ spend much time with us. ☐ don't ☐ doesn't

I0   _____ your friends live near here? ☐ Do ☐ Does

box 안의 예문을 참고하여 우리말과 일치하도록 문장을 완성하시오.

WRITING POINT ①

- I **don't study** at night. 나는 / 공부하지 않는다 / 밤에는
- She **doesn't drink** coffee. 그녀는 / 마시지 않는다 / 커피를

---

1 나는 아침을 먹지 않는다.
   I _____ _____ breakfast.

2 너는 채소를 좋아하지 않는다.
   You _____ _____ vegetables.

3 그는 차를 운전하지 않는다.
   He _____ _____ a car.

4 그녀는 안경을 쓰지 않는다.
   She _____ _____ glasses.

5 우리는 오늘 수업이 없다.
   We _____ _____ classes today.

6 그들은 이 거리에 살지 않는다.
   They _____ _____ on this street.

7 Kelly는 옷을 많이 사지 않는다.
   Kelly _____ _____ many clothes.

8 그 버스는 여기에 서지 않는다.
   The bus _____ _____ here.

WRITING POINT ②

- **Do you like** Chinese food? 너는 / 좋아하니 / 중국 음식을?
- **Does he exercise** every day? 그는 / 운동을 하니 / 매일?

---

1 너는 그의 이름을 아니?
   _____ you _____ his name?

2 그는 드럼을 연주하니?
   _____ he _____ the drums?

3 그녀는 불어를 말하니?
   _____ she _____ French?

4 우리는 시간이 더 필요하나요?
   _____ we _____ more time?

5 그들은 토요일에 일하니?
   _____ they _____ on Saturday?

6 Nora는 자매가 있니?
   _____ Nora _____ a sister?

7 Andrew와 Mary는 개들을 좋아하니?
   _____ Andrew and Mary _____ dogs?

8 너희 아버지는 종종 요리를 하시니?
   _____ your father often _____?

우리말과 일치하도록 빈칸에 알맞은 말을 넣으시오.

• 일반동사의 부정문 •

I   나는 그에 대해서 많이 알지 못한다. (know)

→ _____ _____ _____ much about him.

2   호주에는 눈이 내리지 않는다. (it)

→ _____ _____ _____ in Australia.

3   우리에게는 시간이 많지 않다. (have)

→ _____ _____ _____ much time.

4   그 식당은 아침 식사를 제공하지 않는다. (the restaurant / serve)

→ _____ _____ _____ _____ breakfast.

5   Judy와 Frank는 한국어를 잘하지 못한다. (Korean)

→ _____ _____ _____ _____ _____ _____ well.

• 일반동사의 의문문 •

6   너는 악기를 다루니? (play)

→ _____ _____ _____ a musical instrument?

7   그는 매일 체육관에 가니? (the gym)

→ _____ _____ _____ _____ _____ every day?

8   너희 아버지는 양복을 입고 출근하시니? (wear / a suit)

→ _____ _____ _____ _____ _____ to work?

9   Tara와 Dave는 여행을 많이 하니? (travel)

→ _____ _____ _____ _____ _____ a lot?

I0   여름 방학은 7월에 시작하니? (the summer vacation / start)

→ _____ _____ _____ _____ in July?

TRY WRITING

( ) 안의 말을 이용하여 우리말을 영어로 옮기시오.

1 그는 거짓말을 하지 않는다. (tell lies)

2 나는 더운 날씨를 좋아하지 않는다. (hot weather)

3 너는 저녁 식사 후에 산책을 하니? (take a walk / after dinner)

4 그 컴퓨터는 잘 작동하지 않는다. (work well)

5 너는 매일 아침 침대를 정리하니? (make your bed)

6 이 버스는 공항까지 갑니까? (the airport)

7 그 아이들은 행복하지 않다. (the children / feel happy)

8 그들은 중고품을 팔지 않는다. (used things)

9 이 선생님(Mr. Lee)은 과학을 가르치시니? (science)

10 John은 학교에 친구들이 많지 않다. (many / at school)

11 6월에는 비가 많이 오니? (it / a lot / in June)

12 당신 나라의 사람들은 젓가락을 사용하나요? (people in your country / chopsticks)

1 주어진 단어를 이용하여 다음 대화의 밑줄 친 우리말을 영작하시오.

> **A** What do you usually do in your free time?
> **B** 나는 도서관에 가. (to the library)

→ _____

2 주어진 우리말을 참고하여 대화를 완성하시오.

> **A** _____ _____ _____
> in Japan? (그들은 일본에 살고 있니?)
> **B** No, _____ _____ .
> _____ _____ in Seoul.
> (아니, 그렇지 않아. 그들은 서울에 살아.)

3 다음 문장을 지시에 따라 바꾸어 쓰시오.

> We have a math test today.

(1) (부정문으로)
→ _____

(2) (의문문으로)
→ _____

4 ( ) 안에 주어진 동사의 알맞은 형태를 쓰시오.

> Sujin has a busy day every day. She (1) _____ (get) up at 6 in the morning. And she (2) _____ (have) breakfast at 7. She (3) _____ (leave) home for school at around 8. She (4) _____ (arrive) at school at about 8:30.

5 그림을 보고 두 사람을 설명하는 문장을 완성하시오.

→ The girl has a cat, but the boy _____ _____ a cat. He has a dog.

6 다음은 수진이의 일과표이다. 표를 보고 수진이에 관한 문장을 현재시제를 이용하여 완성하시오.

3 p.m.	take a piano lesson
5 p.m.	go to the gym
8 p.m.	do her homework

(1) Sujin _____ at 3 p.m.
(2) Sujin _____ at 5 p.m.
(3) Sujin _____ at 8 p.m.

7 밑줄 친 ①~⑤에서 어법상 틀린 곳을 2개 찾아 바르게 고쳐 쓰시오.

> **A** ① Do your father ② work in Seoul?
> **B** No, he ③ doesn't. He ④ work in Busan. So I ⑤ don't see him very often.

_____ → _____
_____ → _____

UNIT 03

시제

be동사의 과거형

1 과거시제는 과거의 일이나 상태를 나타낸다. **be동사의 과거형**은 was, were로 '~이었다', '(~에) 있었다'란 뜻이다.

주어	be동사 과거형	예
I / He / She / It / 단수명사	was	I was at home yesterday. 나는 어제 집에 있었다. Ms. Kim was our teacher. 김 선생님은 우리 선생님이었다.
We / You / They / 복수명사	were	We were tired last night. 우리는 어젯밤 피곤했다. The trees were small. 그 나무들은 작았다.

> **PLUS** 과거시제는 주로 과거를 나타내는 부사(구)와 함께 쓴다.
> e.g. yesterday(어제), last ~(지난 ~), ~ ago(~ 전에), in 2007(2007년에), then(그때) 등

2 be동사 과거형의 부정문과 의문문

부정문	was/were + not	The party was not[wasn't] fun. 그 파티는 재미있지 않았다. We were not[weren't] busy last week. 우리는 지난주에 바쁘지 않았다.
의문문	Was/Were + 주어 ~?	Was he born in Korea? 그는 한국에서 태어났니? Were they at the beach? 그들은 해변에 있었니?

> **NOTE** be동사 과거형의 의문문에 대한 답은 「Yes, 주어+was/were.」, 「No, 주어+wasn't/weren't.」로 한다.
> e.g. Was the food good? – Yes, it was. / No, it wasn't.
> Were the boys your classmates? – Yes, they were. / No, they weren't.

CHECK UP

● 빈칸에 알맞은 be동사의 과거형을 고르시오.

1 I _____ eleven years old last year. ☐ was ☐ were

2 We _____ in the library yesterday. ☐ was not ☐ were not

3 _____ you late for class this morning? ☐ Was ☐ Were

4 It _____ cold last weekend. ☐ was not ☐ were not

5 Bob _____ a member of the Baduk club. ☐ was ☐ were

6 _____ Tom and Lisa in your class? ☐ Was ☐ Were

7 The books _____ on the desk. ☐ was not ☐ were not

8 _____ the basketball game exciting? ☐ Was ☐ Were

9 His clothes _____ completely wet. ☐ was ☐ were

box 안의 예문을 참고하여 우리말과 일치하도록 문장을 완성하시오.

WRITING POINT ①

- I **was** sick yesterday. 나는 / 이었다 / 아픈 / 어제
- They **were** soccer players. 그들은 / 이었다 / 축구 선수

1 나는 어제 바빴다.

I _____ busy yesterday.

2 나의 어머니는 간호사였다.

My mother _____ a nurse.

3 Sam과 나는 같은 반이었다.

Sam and I _____ in the same class.

4 우리는 오늘 아침에 학교에 늦었다.

We _____ late for school this morning.

5 그들은 지난 일요일에 교회에 있었다.

They _____ at church last Sunday.

WRITING POINT ②

- He **wasn't** at school yesterday. 그는 / 없었다 / 학교에 / 어제
- We **weren't** students in 2000. 우리는 / 아니었다 / 학생이 / 2000년에

1 그는 2010년에 런던에 없었다.

He _____ in London in 2010.

2 그들은 피곤하지 않았다.

They _____ tired.

3 그 시험은 어렵지 않았다.

The exam _____ difficult.

4 그 아이들은 조용하지 않았다.

The children _____ quiet.

WRITING POINT ③

- **Was** she angry with you? 이었니 / 그녀는 / 화난 (화났니?)
- **Were** you at the concert? 있었니 / 너는 / 콘서트에?

1 그는 네 친구였니?

_____ he your friend?

2 너는 지난 주말에 집에 있었니?

_____ you at home last weekend?

3 그 호텔은 편안했니?

_____ the hotel comfortable?

4 그 소년들은 공원에 있었니?

_____ the boys in the park?

우리말과 일치하도록 빈칸에 알맞은 말을 넣으시오.

• be동사의 과거형: 긍정문 •

I   어제는 춥고 바람이 불었다. (cold / windy)

→ It ＿＿＿＿＿ ＿＿＿＿＿ ＿＿＿＿＿ ＿＿＿＿＿ yesterday.

2   내 여동생은 5월에 태어났다. (born)

→ ＿＿＿＿＿ ＿＿＿＿＿ ＿＿＿＿＿ ＿＿＿＿＿ in May.

3   우리는 작년 여름에 시드니에 있었다. (in Sydney)

→ ＿＿＿＿＿ ＿＿＿＿＿ ＿＿＿＿＿ ＿＿＿＿＿ last summer.

4   프랑크푸르트는 독일의 수도였다. (the capital of Germany)

→ Frankfurt ＿＿＿＿＿ ＿＿＿＿＿ ＿＿＿＿＿ ＿＿＿＿＿ ＿＿＿＿＿.

• be동사의 과거형: 부정문 •

5   그들은 서로 친하지 않았다. (close)

→ ＿＿＿＿＿ ＿＿＿＿＿ ＿＿＿＿＿ to each other.

6   그 우산은 차 안에 없었다. (the umbrella)

→ ＿＿＿＿＿ ＿＿＿＿＿ ＿＿＿＿＿ in the car.

7   Lucy와 나는 같은 반이 아니었다.

→ ＿＿＿＿＿ ＿＿＿＿＿ ＿＿＿＿＿ ＿＿＿＿＿ in the same class.

• be동사의 과거형: 의문문 •

8   그는 대학에서 교수였나요? (a professor)

→ ＿＿＿＿＿ ＿＿＿＿＿ ＿＿＿＿＿ at a university?

9   어젯밤 그 영화는 좋았니? (the movie / good)

→ ＿＿＿＿＿ ＿＿＿＿＿ ＿＿＿＿＿ last night?

10   John과 Peggy는 네 생일 파티에 있었니?

→ ＿＿＿＿＿ ＿＿＿＿＿ ＿＿＿＿＿ ＿＿＿＿＿ at your birthday party?

( ) 안의 말을 이용하여 우리말을 영어로 옮기시오.

1 그 책은 내 침대 밑에 있었다. (under)

2 David Beckham은 내가 가장 좋아하는 축구 선수였다. (favorite soccer player)

3 Picasso와 Van Gogh는 위대한 화가였다. (great artists)

4 그것은 내 실수였어. (it / mistake)

5 고등학교 때 수학을 잘하셨어요? (good at / in high school)

6 다행히도, 우리는 학교에 늦지 않았다. (luckily / late for school)

7 나는 그 시험이 끝나고 피곤했다. (after the exam)

8 그 파티는 재미있지 않았다. 그것은 지루했다. (fun / boring)

9 나의 부모님과 나는 지난주에 휴가 중이었다. (on vacation)

10 그는 2016년에 뉴욕에 있었니? (in New York / in 2016)

11 그들은 어젯밤에 극장에 있었니? (at the theater)

12 그는 그 당시에 유명한 가수가 아니었다. (a famous singer / at the time)

LESSON 06 일반동사의 과거형

| 일반동사의 과거형은 대부분의 동사에 **-ed**를 붙여 만든다. 이외에 **had**(가지고 있었다), **went**(갔다), **bought**(샀다)처럼 불규칙하게 변하는 동사들은 암기해야 한다.

규칙 동사	대부분의 동사	+ ed	listen**ed**, clean**ed**, walk**ed**, play**ed**
	-e로 끝나는 동사	+ d	lived, closed, invited, saved
	「자음 + y」로 끝나는 동사	y → i + ed	stud**ied**, tr**ied**, cr**ied**, carr**ied**
	「단모음 + 단자음」으로 끝나는 동사	마지막 자음 추가 + ed	stop**ped**, plan**ned**, drop**ped**, jog**ged**
불규칙 동사	cut-**cut**, do-**did**, go-**went**, eat-**ate**, write-**wrote** 등		

They **walked** to school this morning. 그들은 오늘 아침 학교에 걸어갔다.
She **wrote** the book in 2007. 그녀는 그 책을 2007년에 썼다.

2 일반동사 과거형의 부정문과 의문문

부정문	did not[didn't] + 동사원형	They played tennis yesterday. → They did not[didn't] play tennis yesterday. 그들은 어제 테니스를 치지 않았다.
의문문	Did + 주어 + 동사원형 ~?	You met Susan last week? → Did you meet Susan last week? 너는 지난주에 Susan을 만났니?

NOTE 일반동사 과거형의 의문문에 대한 답은 「Yes, 주어 + did.」, 「No, 주어 + didn't.」로 한다.
e.g. Did you sleep well last night? – *Yes*, I *did. / No*, I *didn't*.

CHECK UP

● 주어진 동사를 과거형으로 바꿔 쓰시오.

| learn   _____   **9** go   _____

2 want   _____   **10** eat   _____

3 pass   _____   **||** read   _____

4 love   _____   **12** see   _____

5 cry   _____   **13** hear   _____

6 enjoy   _____   **14** know   _____

7 stop   _____   **15** write   _____

8 plan   _____   **16** buy   _____

SENTENCE PRACTICE 1

box 안의 예문을 참고하여 우리말과 일치하도록 문장을 완성하시오.

WRITING POINT ①

• He **helped** sick people. 그는 / 도와주었다 / 아픈 사람들을

1 우리는 집에 일찍 갔다.　　　　　　We _____ home early.

2 그는 그 시험에 합격했다.　　　　　He _____ the exam.

3 하루 종일 비가 왔다.　　　　　　　It _____ all day.

4 Kevin은 그 꽃병을 깨뜨렸다.　　　Kevin _____ the vase.

5 나는 내 우산을 잃어버렸다.　　　　I _____ my umbrella.

WRITING POINT ②

• I **didn't watch** the movie. 나는 / 보지 않았다 / 그 영화를

1 나는 너에게 전화하지 않았다.　　　I _____ _____ you.

2 그는 그 셔츠를 사지 않았다.　　　　He _____ _____ the shirt.

3 그녀는 그 음식을 먹지 않았다.　　　She _____ _____ the food.

4 우리는 그 소식을 듣지 않았다.　　　We _____ _____ the news.

5 그들은 그 창문을 닫지 않았다.　　　They _____ _____ the window.

WRITING POINT ③

• **Did you walk** to school this morning? 너는 / 걸어갔니 / 학교에 / 오늘 아침?

1 그는 운전해서 출근했니?　　　　　_____ he _____ to work?

2 너는 네 열쇠를 찾았니?　　　　　　_____ you _____ your key?

3 그는 그 컴퓨터를 고쳤니?　　　　　_____ he _____ the computer?

4 그녀는 숙제를 끝냈니?　　　　　　_____ she _____ her homework?

5 그들은 그 경기에서 이겼니?　　　　_____ they _____ the game?

우리말과 일치하도록 빈칸에 알맞은 말을 넣으시오.

• 일반동사의 과거형: 긍정문 •

1 우리는 지난 금요일에 영화를 보러 갔다. (go to the movies)

→ _____ _____ _____ _____ last Friday.

2 Brown 씨는 우리를 저녁 식사에 초대했다. (invite)

→ _____ _____ _____ _____ to dinner.

3 그녀는 점심으로 햄버거를 먹었다. (have / a hamburger)

→ _____ _____ _____ _____ for lunch.

4 나는 내 가방을 버스에 두고 내렸다. (leave)

→ _____ _____ _____ _____ on the bus.

• 일반동사의 과거형: 부정문 •

5 그는 먹기 전에 손을 씻지 않았다. (his hands)

→ He _____ _____ _____ _____ before eating.

6 그들은 내 생일파티에 오지 않았다. (come to)

→ They _____ _____ _____ my birthday party.

7 그 스테이크는 맛이 좋지 않았다. (taste good)

→ The steak _____ _____ _____ .

• 일반동사의 과거형: 의문문 •

8 그는 영국에 살았었니? (live)

→ _____ _____ _____ in England?

9 그녀가 에어컨을 켰니? (turn on)

→ _____ _____ _____ _____ the air conditioner?

10 너는 식사 후에 이를 닦았니? (brush your teeth)

→ _____ _____ _____ _____ _____ after the meal?

( ) 안의 말을 이용하여 우리말을 영어로 옮기시오.

I   Chris는 새 기타를 샀다. (a new guitar)

2   우리는 지난 주말에 쇼핑을 갔다. (go shopping)

3   내가 실수를 저질렀니? (make a mistake)

4   Rick은 어제 그의 숙제를 깜박했다. (forget)

5   그들은 휴일을 즐겼니? (their holiday)

6   Brad와 Angela는 2014년에 결혼했다. (get married)

7   너는 오늘 아침에 식사를 걸렀니? (skip breakfast)

8   그 기차는 정시에 도착하지 않았다. (on time)

9   Lucy는 지난주에 친구들을 만나지 않았다. (her friends)

IO Lisa는 미술 시간에 손가락을 베었다. (cut her finger / in art class)

II Steve는 어젯밤에 잠을 잘 자지 못했다. (sleep well)

I2 나의 형은 백일장에서 1등 상을 받았다. (win the first prize / in the writing contest)

LESSON 07 현재진행형

1 현재진행형은 지금 일어나는 일을 표현한다. 형태는 「am/are/is＋동사원형＋-ing」이고, '~하고 있다, ~하는 중이다'란 뜻이다.

I **am eating** dinner. 나는 저녁을 먹고 있다.
The baby **is sleeping**. 그 아기는 잠을 자고 있다.
They **are washing** the dishes. 그들은 설거지를 하고 있다.

2 현재진행형의 부정문과 의문문

부정문	am/are/is + not + -ing	I am not reading a book. 나는 책을 읽고 있지 않다.
의문문	Am/Are/Is + 주어 + -ing ~?	Are you doing your homework? 너는 숙제를 하고 있니?

3 현재시제 vs. 현재진행형
일반적인 사실, 반복되는 습관이나 행위는 현재시제로 표현하고, 지금 일어나고 있는 일은 현재진행형을 쓴다.

I **take** a shower every morning. 나는 매일 아침 샤워를 한다.
I **am taking** a shower now. 나는 지금 샤워 중이다.

CHECK UP

● 빈칸에 알맞은 말을 고르시오.

1 We usually _____ three meals a day. ☐ eat ☐ are eating

2 Many people _____ for the bus now. ☐ wait ☐ are waiting

3 She _____ to church on Saturday. ☐ goes ☐ is going

4 Anna _____ apple pie right now. ☐ makes ☐ is making

5 I _____ my grandparents once a month. ☐ visit ☐ am visiting

6 Two people _____ under the tree. ☐ sit ☐ are sitting

7 Look! It _____ outside. ☐ snows ☐ is snowing

8 The hen _____ an egg every day. ☐ lays ☐ is laying

9 Sarah and David _____ home. ☐ come ☐ are coming

10 I _____ a glass of milk every morning. ☐ drink ☐ am drinking

box 안의 예문을 참고하여 우리말과 일치하도록 문장을 완성하시오.

WRITING POINT 1

· He **is running** along the river. 그는 / 달리고 있다 / 강을 따라

1 그들은 해변을 따라 걷고 있다.　　　　They ＿＿＿＿＿ ＿＿＿＿＿ along the beach.

2 그 소녀는 벤치에 앉아 있다.　　　　　The girl ＿＿＿＿＿ ＿＿＿＿＿ on the bench.

3 그 소년들은 자전거를 타고 있다.　　　The boys ＿＿＿＿＿ ＿＿＿＿＿ bicycles.

4 내 고양이는 소파 위에서 자고 있다.　　My cat ＿＿＿＿＿ ＿＿＿＿＿ on the sofa.

5 밖에는 비가 내리고 있다.　　　　　　It ＿＿＿＿＿ ＿＿＿＿＿ outside.

WRITING POINT 2

· I'**m not watching** TV at the moment. 나는 / 보고 있지 않다 / TV를 / 지금

1 그녀는 운전을 하고 있지 않다.　　　　She ＿＿＿＿＿ ＿＿＿＿＿ a car.

2 너는 안경을 쓰고 있지 않다.　　　　　You ＿＿＿＿＿ ＿＿＿＿＿ glasses.

3 Julie는 지금 요리를 하고 있지 않다.　　Julie ＿＿＿＿＿ ＿＿＿＿＿ now.

4 그 기차는 지금 달리고 있지 않다.　　　The train ＿＿＿＿＿ ＿＿＿＿＿ now.

5 그들은 통화하고 있지 않다.　　　　　They ＿＿＿＿＿ ＿＿＿＿＿ on the phone.

WRITING POINT 3

· **Are you listening** to me? 너는 / 듣고 있니 / 내 말을?

1 그는 TV를 보고 있니?　　　　　　　＿＿＿＿＿ he ＿＿＿＿＿ TV?

2 그녀는 책을 읽고 있니?　　　　　　　＿＿＿＿＿ she ＿＿＿＿＿ a book?

3 너는 즐거운 시간을 보내고 있니?　　　＿＿＿＿＿ you ＿＿＿＿＿ a good time?

4 그들은 배구를 하고 있니?　　　　　　＿＿＿＿＿ they ＿＿＿＿＿ volleyball?

5 Kevin과 Lisa는 숙제를 하고 있니?　　　＿＿＿＿＿ Kevin and Lisa ＿＿＿＿＿ their homework?

우리말과 일치하도록 빈칸에 알맞은 말을 넣으시오.

• 현재진행형: 긍정문 •

1 나는 내 고양이에게 밥을 주고 있다. (feed)

→ I _____ _____ _____ _____.

2 그 아이들은 길을 건너고 있다. (cross the street)

→ The children _____ _____ _____ _____.

3 Robin은 지금 침대에 누워 있다. (lie in bed)

→ Robin _____ _____ _____ _____ now.

4 손님들은 그들의 코트를 벗고 있다. (take off)

→ The guests _____ _____ _____ _____.

• 현재진행형: 부정문 •

5 Sarah는 귀걸이를 하고 있지 않다. (earrings)

→ Sarah _____ _____ _____.

6 너는 나에게 진실을 말하고 있지 않아. (tell me the truth)

→ You _____ _____ _____ _____ _____.

7 에스컬레이터는 지금 작동하지 않는다. (work)

→ The escalator _____ _____ at the moment.

• 현재진행형: 의문문 •

8 너는 도서관에서 공부하고 있니? (study)

→ _____ _____ _____ in the library?

9 그들은 지금 전화 통화 중이니? (talk on the phone)

→ _____ _____ _____ _____ _____ _____ now?

10 Jane은 그녀 방에서 바이올린을 연습하고 있니? (practice the violin)

→ _____ _____ _____ _____ _____ in her room?

( ) 안의 말을 이용하여 우리말을 영어로 옮기시오.

1 그녀는 차 한잔을 마시고 있다. (a cup of tea)

2 너는 너무 큰 소리로 노래 부르고 있어. (too loudly)

3 그는 복사기를 사용 중이니? (the copy machine)

4 나는 오늘 몸이 좋지 않다. (feel well)

5 나의 아버지는 지금 은행에서 일하고 있지 않다. (at a bank / now)

6 Helen은 전통 한국 음식을 요리하고 있다. (a traditional Korean food)

7 너는 네 차 열쇠를 찾고 있니? (look for / car keys)

8 한 이상한 남자가 나를 빤히 쳐다보고 있다. (stare at)

9 우진(Woojin)은 지금 뜨거운 물에 목욕을 하고 있다. (take a hot bath / right now)

10 너는 네 휴대전화를 충전 중이니? (charge)

11 나의 할머니는 정원에서 꽃에 물을 주고 계신다. (water the flowers)

12 Tom과 Rachael은 통학 버스를 기다리고 있니? (wait for / the school bus)

1 우리말과 같은 뜻이 되도록 빈칸에 알맞은 말을 쓰시오.

(1) 나는 작년에 2학년이었다.

→ I _____ in the second grade last year.

(2) 너는 어제 도서관에 있었니?

→ _____ you in the library yesterday?

(3) Emily와 나는 친한 친구가 아니었다.

→ Emily and I _____ close friends.

2 다음은 Mike의 일과표이다. 표를 보고 주어진 질문에 알맞은 답을 완전한 문장으로 쓰시오.

3:00 - 4:30 p.m.	study in class
4:30 - 5:30 p.m.	take a taekwondo lesson
5:30 - 6:30 p.m.	eat dinner

Q It is 5 o'clock in the afternoon. What is Mike doing now?

A _____

3 다음 문장을 지시에 따라 바꾸어 쓰시오.

My dad makes dinner for us.

(1) (현재진행형으로)

→ _____

(2) (과거형으로)

→ _____

4 주어진 단어를 이용하여 우리말을 영작하시오. (단, 과거시제를 사용할 것)

(1) 그는 그 시험에 합격하지 못했다.
(pass the exam)

→ _____

(2) 너는 그 소설을 읽었니? (the novel)

→ _____

5 그림을 보고 질문에 대한 답을 완성하시오. (단, 주어진 단어를 이용하여 8단어로 쓸 것)

Q What is Jane doing now?

A She _____

_____. (play, a song)

6 그림을 보고 질문에 대한 답을 완성하시오.

Q What did you buy at the market?

A _____ _____ some

_____ and _____.

7 다음은 Wendy가 지난 일요일에 쓴 일기이다. 〈조건〉에 맞게 일기를 완성하시오.

조건 1. go / be / eat / wake up / take / meet 를 모두 사용할 것
2. 단어의 형태를 어법에 맞게 쓸 것

I (1)_____ early this morning. I (2)_____ a walk in the park. At noon, I (3)_____ my friends. We (4)_____ pizza for lunch. I (5)_____ tired, so I (6)_____ to bed early.

UNIT
04

조동사

LESSON 08 will, be going to

1 조동사 **will**은 '~할 것이다'란 뜻으로, **미래의 예측**이나 **의지**를 나타낸다.

긍정문	will['ll] + 동사원형	**It'll rain** all this week. 이번 주 내내 비가 올 것이다.
부정문	will not[won't] + 동사원형	She **will not[won't] watch** TV tonight. 그녀는 오늘 밤에 TV를 보지 않을 것이다.
의문문	Will + 주어 + 동사원형 ~?	A: **Will they come** tomorrow? 그들은 내일 올 거니? B: Yes, they will. / No, they won't.

2 **be going to**는 '~할 것이다, ~할 예정이다'란 뜻으로, **미래의 예측**이나 **계획**을 나타낸다.

긍정문	be going to + 동사원형	I **am going to read** the book. 나는 그 책을 읽을 것이다.
부정문	be동사 + not + going to + 동사원형	He **is not going to meet** Sara next week. 그는 다음 주에 Sara를 만나지 않을 것이다.
의문문	Be동사 + 주어 + going to + 동사원형 ~?	A: **Are you going to go** fishing? 너는 낚시하러 갈 거니? B: Yes, I am. / No, I am not.

PLUS will vs. be going to
will과 be going to는 모두 미래의 예측을 나타내지만, 말하는 순간 내린 결정에는 will을, 사전 계획에는 be going to 만을 쓴다.
e.g. A: This box is too heavy. B: Wait, I'*ll* help you.
A: What *are* you *going to* do tomorrow? B: I'*m going to* visit my aunt.

CHECK UP

● 빈칸에 알맞은 말을 고르시오.

1	We will _____ you soon.	☐ see	☐ saw
2	Will you _____ here on Wednesday?	☐ is	☐ be
3	They are not going _____ tennis on Saturday.	☐ play	☐ to play
4	Philip will _____ us home.	☐ drive	☐ drives
5	This weekend I am going _____ Eva.	☐ meeting	☐ to meet
6	Is he going _____ to Japan tomorrow?	☐ flies	☐ to fly
7	The new hotel will not _____ this summer.	☐ open	☐ to open
8	Jill is going _____ a surprise party for Ann.	☐ having	☐ to have
9	What will you _____ after you graduate?	☐ do	☐ doing
10	Hurry up, or we are going _____ late.	☐ being	☐ to be

box 안의 예문을 참고하여 우리말과 일치하도록 문장을 완성하시오.

WRITING POINT ❶

- You **will go** to the concert. 너는 / 갈 것이다 / 콘서트에
- You **will not go** to the concert. 너는 / 가지 않을 것이다 / 콘서트에
- **Will you go** to the concert? 너는 갈 거니 / 콘서트에?

1 나는 오늘 저녁에 집에 있을 것이다. I _____ at home this evening.

2 나는 오늘 저녁에 집에 없을 것이다. I _____ at home this evening.

3 그는 정오에 점심을 먹을 것이다. He _____ lunch at noon.

4 그는 정오에 점심을 먹지 않을 것이다. He _____ lunch at noon.

5 그들은 내 파티에 올 것이다. They _____ to my party.

6 그들은 내 파티에 올 거니? _____ to my party?

7 Susan은 이 선물을 좋아할 것이다. Susan _____ this present.

8 Susan은 이 선물을 좋아할까? _____ this present?

WRITING POINT ❷

- He **is going to buy** a new car. 그는 / 살 것이다 / 새 차를
- He **isn't going to buy** a new car. 그는 / 사지 않을 것이다 / 새 차를
- **Is he going to buy** a new car? 그는 살 거니 / 새 차를?

1 우리는 그것을 할 것이다. We _____ it.

2 우리는 그것을 하지 않을 것이다. We _____ it.

3 나는 그 영화를 볼 것이다. I _____ the movie.

4 나는 그 영화를 보지 않을 것이다. I _____ the movie.

5 그들은 박물관에 방문할 것이다. They _____ the museum.

6 그들은 박물관에 방문할 거니? _____ the museum?

7 Mike는 회의에 올 것이다. Mike _____ to the meeting.

8 Mike는 회의에 올 거니? _____ to the meeting?

우리말과 일치하도록 빈칸에 알맞은 말을 넣으시오.

• will •

1 우리는 기다리면서 지켜볼 것이다. (wait / see)

→ We _____ _____ _____ _____.

2 Eric은 우리를 역까지 차로 태워다 줄 것이다. (drive)

→ Eric _____ _____ _____ to the station.

3 나는 버스를 타지 않을 것이다. 걸어갈 것이다. (take / walk)

→ I _____ _____ _____ a bus. I _____ _____.

4 몇몇 사람들은 이것을 믿지 않을 것이다. (believe)

→ Some people _____ _____ _____ this.

5 너는 오늘 저녁에 집에 있을 거니? (be / at home)

→ _____ _____ _____ _____ _____ this evening?

• be going to •

6 나는 다음 달에 새 집으로 이사할 것이다. (move)

→ I _____ _____ _____ _____ into a new house next month.

7 그는 내일 부산으로 떠날 것이다. (leave for)

→ He _____ _____ _____ _____ _____ Busan tomorrow.

8 우리는 오늘 시험을 보지 않을 것이다. (take a test)

→ We _____ _____ _____ _____ _____ today.

9 그들은 이번 주 토요일에 일할 거니? (work)

→ _____ _____ _____ _____ _____ this Saturday?

10 나의 부모님은 오늘 저녁에 외출하지 않을 것이다. (go out)

→ My parents _____ _____ _____ _____ _____ this evening.

( ) 안의 말을 이용하여 우리말을 영어로 옮기시오.

1 나는 최선을 다할 것이다. (will / do my best)

2 우리는 이 오래된 가구를 팔 예정이다. (going to / this old furniture)

3 그들은 다음 달에 결혼 할 예정이다. (going to / get married)

4 너는 장래에 영화 감독이 될 거니? (will / a movie director)

5 그의 아들은 다음 달이면 열다섯 살이 된다. (will / fifteen years old)

6 너는 아무 문제 없을 거야. (will / any problems)

7 너는 파티에 저 드레스를 입을 거니? (going to / that dress / to the party)

8 그들은 내일 떠나지 않을 것이다. (going to / leave)

9 Ted는 7월에 비행기로 런던에 갈 것이다. (going to / fly to / in July)

10 나는 5분 후에 준비가 될 것이다. (will / be ready / in five minutes)

11 우리는 멋진 식당에서 저녁을 먹을 것이다. (going to / at a nice restaurant)

12 미래에, 사람들은 다른 행성으로 여행을 갈 것이다. (will / travel to / other planets)

can, may

I 조동사 can은 '~할 수 있다'라는 **능력**과 '~해도 좋다', '~해도 되나요?'라는 **허락**의 의미를 나타낸다.

능력	I can speak English well. 나는 영어를 잘 말할 수 있다. Penguins cannot[can't] fly. 펭귄들은 날 수 없다.
허락	You can sit here. 여기 앉아도 좋아. Can I ask a favor? 부탁 하나 해도 될까요?

PLUS 상대방에게 '~해줄 수 있니?'라고 요청할 때는 'Can you ~?'로 묻는다.
e.g. *Can you* open the door? 문 좀 열어줄 수 있니?

2 조동사 may는 '~일지도 모른다'라는 **추측**과 '~해도 좋다', '~해도 되나요?'라는 **허락**의 의미를 나타낸다.

추측	It may rain tomorrow. 내일은 비가 올지도 모른다. The rumor may not be true. 그 소문은 사실이 아닐지도 모른다.
허락	You may/can leave now. 너는 이제 가도 좋다. May/Can I come in? 제가 들어가도 될까요?

PLUS can, may가 허락을 뜻하는 의문문으로 쓰였을 때 응답
- 수락의 표현: Yes, you can/may. / Sure. / Of course. / No problem. / Okay.
- 거절의 표현: No, you can't/may not. / Sorry. / I'm sorry.

CHECK UP

● 밑줄 친 조동사의 의미를 고르시오.

I Jane <u>can</u> play the piano.　　　　　☐ 능력　　☐ 허락

2 <u>May</u> I see your ticket, please?　　　☐ 추측　　☐ 허락

3 The baby <u>cannot</u> walk yet.　　　　☐ 능력　　☐ 추측

4 It <u>may</u> be sunny tomorrow.　　　　☐ 추측　　☐ 허락

5 <u>Can</u> you swim in the sea?　　　　　☐ 능력　　☐ 추측

6 You <u>may</u> use my cell phone.　　　　☐ 추측　　☐ 허락

7 <u>Can</u> I borrow your notebook?　　　☐ 능력　　☐ 허락

8 He <u>may not</u> know my name.　　　☐ 추측　　☐ 허락

9 My grandfather <u>can't</u> hear well.　　☐ 능력　　☐ 허락

I0 You <u>may</u> use this room if you want.　☐ 추측　　☐ 허락

box 안의 예문을 참고하여 우리말과 일치하도록 문장을 완성하시오.

> **WRITING POINT ①**
>
> • I **can play** the violin. 나는 / 연주할 수 있다 / 바이올린을
> • I **cannot play** the violin. 나는 / 연주할 수 없다 / 바이올린을
> • **Can you play** the violin? 너는 연주할 수 있니 / 바이올린을?

1 나는 그 노래를 부를 수 있다.　　　　I _____ the song.

2 나는 그 노래를 부를 수 없다.　　　　I _____ the song.

3 그는 지금 전화를 받을 수 있다.　　　He _____ the phone right now.

4 그는 지금 전화를 받을 수 없다.　　　He _____ the phone right now.

5 우리는 도서관을 이용할 수 있다.　　We _____ the library.

6 우리가 도서관을 이용할 수 있나요?　_____ the library?

7 Judy는 자전거를 탈 수 있다.　　　　Judy _____ a bicycle.

8 Judy는 자전거를 탈 수 있니?　　　　_____ a bicycle?

> **WRITING POINT ②**
>
> • He **may come** today. 그는 / 올지도 모른다 / 오늘
> • He **may not come** today. 그는 / 오지 않을지도 모른다 / 오늘
> • **May I leave** a message? 제가 남겨도 될까요 / 메시지를?

1 나는 시험에 합격할지도 모른다.　　　I _____ the exam.

2 나는 시험에 합격하지 않을지도 모른다.　I _____ the exam.

3 그는 오늘 아픈지도 몰라.　　　　　　He _____ sick today.

4 그는 오늘 아프지 않을지도 몰라　　　He _____ sick today.

5 너는 내일 내 차를 사용해도 좋다.　　You _____ my car tomorrow.

6 너는 내일 내 차를 사용해서는 안 된다.　You _____ my car tomorrow.

7 여기 앉아도 될까요?　　　　　　　　_____ here?

8 질문 하나 해도 될까요?　　　　　　　_____ a question?

우리말과 일치하도록 빈칸에 알맞은 말을 넣으시오.

• can •

1 그녀는 영어를 잘할 수 있다. (speak)

→ _____ _____ _____ _____ well.

2 우리는 물 없이 살 수 없다. (live)

→ _____ _____ _____ without water.

3 네가 나에게 이럴 수는 없어. (do)

→ _____ _____ _____ this to me.

4 내 숙제 좀 도와줄 수 있니? (help)

→ _____ _____ _____ me with my homework?

5 Tom은 수영과 탁구를 아주 잘 할 수 있다. (swim / play table tennis)

→ Tom _____ _____ and _____ _____ _____ very well.

• may •

6 제가 도와드릴까요? (help)

→ _____ _____ _____ you?

7 다음 주에는 눈이 올지도 모른다. (it)

→ _____ _____ _____ next week.

8 그녀는 해산물을 좋아하지 않을 수도 있다. (like)

→ _____ _____ _____ _____ seafood.

9 너는 친구들과 나가도 좋다. (go out)

→ _____ _____ _____ _____ with your friends.

10 여권을 좀 봐도 될까요? (see)

→ _____ _____ _____ your passport?

( ) 안의 말을 이용하여 우리말을 영어로 옮기시오.

1 Dave가 이 차를 고칠 수 있니? (fix)

2 조금 더 크게 말씀해주실 수 있나요? (a little louder)

3 너는 도서관에 있는 컴퓨터들을 사용해도 좋다. (the computers)

4 나는 오늘 밤에 영화 보러 갈지도 모른다. (go to the movies)

5 제가 이 신발을 신어봐도 될까요? (try on / these shoes)

6 어떤 사람들은 3개 국어를 할 수 있다. (some / three languages)

7 나의 할아버지는 안경 없이는 읽을 수 없다. (without glasses)

8 나는 내 열쇠를 어디에서도 찾을 수가 없다. (my key / anywhere)

9 그는 100미터를 12초에 달릴 수 있다. (100 meters / in 12 seconds)

10 네 지갑은 식탁 위에 있을지도 모른다. (your purse / on the table)

11 여기에 주차하시면 안 됩니다. (park / your car)

12 이 박물관에서는 사진을 찍으시면 안 됩니다. (take photos)

LESSON 10 must, have to, should

1 조동사 must는 '~해야 한다'라는 뜻으로 **강한 의무**를 나타낸다. 부정형인 **must not**은 '~해서는 안 된다'라는 **금지**의 의미이다.

의무	must + 동사원형	They **must** obey the rules. 그들은 그 규칙들을 따라야 한다.
금지	must not[mustn't] + 동사원형	You **must not[mustn't]** tell the secret. 너는 그 비밀을 말하면 안 된다.

2 조동사 have/has to는 must처럼 '~해야 한다'라는 **의무**나 **필요**를 나타낸다. 부정형인 **don't/doesn't have to**는 '~할 필요가 없다'라는 **불필요**의 의미이다.

의무/필요	have/has to + 동사원형	I **have to** clean my room. 나는 내 방을 청소해야 한다. She **has to** study tonight. 그녀는 오늘 밤 공부해야 한다.
불필요	don't/doesn't have to + 동사원형	We **don't have to** hurry up. 우리는 서두를 필요 없어.

3 조동사 should는 '~해야 한다, ~하는 게 좋다'라는 **조언**의 뜻을 나타낸다. 부정형인 **should not**은 '~해서는 안 된다, ~하지 않는 게 좋다'라는 의미이다.

조언	should + 동사원형	I **should** study harder. 나는 더 열심히 공부해야 한다.
	should not[shouldn't] + 동사원형	You **should not[shouldn't]** run in the hallway. 복도에서 뛰면 안 된다.

CHECK UP

● 밑줄 친 조동사의 의미를 고르시오.

1 You <u>should</u> brush your teeth after a meal.　　☐ 금지　　☐ 조언

2 He <u>must not</u> break his promise.　　☐ 금지　　☐ 불필요

3 Aron <u>has to</u> do some work.　　☐ 의무/필요　　☐ 조언

4 You <u>should not</u> open the box.　　☐ 불필요　　☐ 조언

5 Drivers <u>must</u> wear seat belts all the time.　　☐ 의무　　☐ 조언

6 He <u>should not</u> watch too much TV.　　☐ 불필요　　☐ 조언

7 Ian <u>doesn't have to</u> go to school today.　　☐ 금지　　☐ 불필요

8 People <u>must</u> keep quiet in the library.　　☐ 의무　　☐ 금지

9 You <u>don't have to</u> wait if I'm late.　　☐ 금지　　☐ 불필요

box 안의 예문을 참고하여 우리말과 일치하도록 문장을 완성하시오.

WRITING POINT ①

- You **must eat** the cake. 너는 / 먹어야 한다 / 그 케이크를
- You **must not eat** the cake. 너는 / 먹으면 안 된다 / 그 케이크를

---

1 너는 진실을 말해야 한다. You _____ the truth.

2 너는 진실을 말하면 안 된다. You _____ the truth.

3 그는 거기에 가야 한다. He _____ there.

4 그는 거기에 가면 안 된다. He _____ there.

WRITING POINT ②

- I **have to wear** a mask. 나는 / 써야 한다 / 마스크를
- I **don't have to wear** a mask. 나는 / 쓸 필요가 없다 / 마스크를

---

1 우리는 그를 기다려야 한다. We _____ for him.

2 우리는 그를 기다릴 필요 없다. We _____ for him.

3 그녀는 택시를 타야 한다. She _____ a taxi.

4 그녀는 택시를 탈 필요가 없다. She _____ a taxi.

WRITING POINT ③

- I **should buy** this coat. 나는 / 사야 한다 / 이 코트를
- I **shouldn't buy** this coat. 나는 / 사면 안 된다 / 이 코트를

---

1 너는 그 영화를 봐야 한다. You _____ the movie.

2 너는 그 영화를 보면 안 된다. You _____ the movie.

3 그들은 늦게까지 일해야 한다. They _____ late.

4 그들은 늦게까지 일하면 안 된다. They _____ late.

SENTENCE PRACTICE 2

우리말과 일치하도록 빈칸에 알맞은 말을 넣으시오.

• must •

1 당신은 모든 질문에 답해야 합니다. (answer)

→ You _____ _____ all the questions.

2 학생들은 내일까지 숙제를 제출해야 한다. (hand in)

→ Students _____ _____ _____ their homework by tomorrow.

3 Jane은 정크푸드를 너무 많이 먹으면 안 된다. (eat)

→ Jane _____ _____ _____ too much junk food.

• have/has to •

4 그는 내일 아침 일찍 일어나야 한다. (get up)

→ He _____ _____ _____ _____ early tomorrow morning.

5 나는 7시까지 집에 있어야 한다. (be home)

→ I _____ _____ _____ _____ by 7 o'clock.

6 사과하실 필요 없습니다. (say sorry)

→ You _____ _____ _____ _____ _____ .

7 Sally는 살을 뺄 필요가 없다. (lose weight)

→ Sally _____ _____ _____ _____ _____ .

• should •

8 너는 규칙적으로 운동을 해야 한다. (exercise regularly)

→ You _____ _____ _____ .

9 그는 너무 늦게까지 깨어 있으면 안 된다. (stay up)

→ He _____ _____ _____ _____ too late.

10 Jake는 그의 가족들과 더 많은 시간을 보내야 한다. (spend)

→ Jake _____ _____ _____ _____ with his family.

( ) 안의 말을 이용하여 우리말을 영어로 옮기시오.

1 너는 네 약속을 지켜야 한다. (must / keep)

2 우리는 매일 충분한 물을 마셔야 한다. (should / enough water)

3 나는 오늘 내 숙제를 끝내야 한다. (have to / finish)

4 사람들은 공공장소에서 담배를 피우면 안 된다. (must / in public places)

5 밤에는 조심해서 운전해야 한다. (should / carefully / at night)

6 너는 그것에 대해 걱정할 필요는 없다. (worry about / it)

7 그들은 그 집을 사면 안 된다. (should)

8 너는 수업 중에 네 휴대전화를 사용하면 안 된다. (must / during the class)

9 너는 하루 세 번 양치질을 해야 한다. (should / three times a day)

10 John은 그의 직업을 위해 영어를 배워야 한다. (have to / for his job)

11 Joe와 Lucy는 그 기차를 타야만 한다. (must / catch)

12 그들은 저녁 식사 값을 낼 필요가 없다. (pay for dinner)

1 두 문장이 같은 의미가 되도록 빈칸에 알맞은 말을 쓰시오.

> It will rain this afternoon.
> = It _____ _____ _____
>   rain this afternoon.

2 다음 문장을 어법에 맞도록 바르게 고쳐 다시 쓰시오.

(1) Will he comes to the party tonight?

→ _____

(2) I'll going to meet Susan this Friday.

→ _____

3 다음 표를 참고하여 아래 질문에 대한 답을 완성하시오.

	Piano	Guitar	Drums
Tom	X	O	X

Q   What musical instrument can Tom play?

A   He _____ .

4 주어진 단어를 이용하여 다음 대화의 밑줄 친 우리말을 영작하시오.

> A Jiho doesn't answer the phone.
> B 그는 집에 없을지도 몰라. (at home)

→ _____

5 우리말과 같은 뜻이 되도록 ( ) 안의 말과 have to를 이용하여 문장을 완성하시오.

(1) 우리는 캔과 병을 재활용해야 한다. (recycle)

→ We _____ cans and bottles.

(2) 너는 우산을 가져갈 필요가 없다. (take)

→ You _____ your umbrella.

6 그림을 보고 주어진 단어와 조동사 must를 이용하여 문장을 완성하시오.

(1) 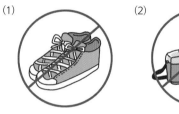　　(2)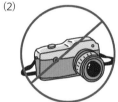

(1) You _____ .
   (take off your shoes)

(2) You _____ .
   (take photos)

7 다음은 교실에서 유의해야 할 사항들이다. 〈보기〉의 표현과 조동사 should를 이용하여 문장을 완성하시오.

보기	talk / be / listen to

(1) You _____ late for class.

(2) You _____ your teacher.

(3) You _____ during the class.

UNIT
05

의문사

LESSON 11

when, where

1 원하는 정보를 묻고자 할 때 when, where, who, what, how, why 등의 의문사를 사용해서 질문할 수 있다.
의문사 when은 '언제'라는 뜻으로 때를 물을 때 쓴다.

| When + be동사 | When + be동사 + 주어 ~? | When is your birthday? 네 생일이 언제니? |
| When + 일반동사 | When + do/does/did + 주어 + 동사원형 ~? | When did you have lunch? 점심 언제 먹었니? |

2 의문사 where는 '어디에'라는 뜻으로 장소를 물을 때 쓴다.

| Where + be동사 | Where + be동사 + 주어 ~? | Where is Susan? Susan은 어디 있니?
Where are you going? 너는 어디 가는 중이니? |
| Where + 일반동사 | Where + do/does/did + 주어 + 동사원형 ~? | Where does he live? 그는 어디에 사니? |

CHECK UP

• 빈칸에 When 또는 Where를 쓰시오.

1 A: _____ is the bathroom?   B: It is on the second floor.

2 A: _____ does he do his laundry?   B: He does it every Saturday.

3 A: _____ do you go swimming?   B: Every morning.

4 A: _____ are Peter and Mike?   B: They are at school.

5 A: _____ is your party?   B: On Friday.

6 A: _____ did you get your first cell phone?   B: It was two years ago.

7 A: _____ were you born?   B: I was born in Seoul.

8 A: _____ did you go for dinner?   B: We went to Ruth's Dining.

9 A: _____ are you going to meet Tara?   B: This Saturday.

10 A: _____ did you find your key?   B: It was in my pocket.

box 안의 예문을 참고하여 우리말과 일치하도록 문장을 완성하시오.

> **WRITING POINT 1**
> • **When is** Korea's Independence Day? 언제니 / 한국의 광복절이?
> • **Where are** my shoes? 어디에 있니 / 내 신발이?

I Jane의 생일이 언제야?　　　　　　　　　　　_____ _____ Jane's birthday?

2 축구 경기는 언제니?　　　　　　　　　　　　_____ _____ the soccer game?

3 너는 어디 출신이니?　　　　　　　　　　　　_____ _____ you from?

4 네 책가방은 어디에 있니?　　　　　　　　　　_____ _____ your school bag?

5 너는 언제 태어났니?　　　　　　　　　　　　_____ _____ you born?

6 그는 어젯밤에 어디에 있었니?　　　　　　　　_____ _____ he last night?

7 그들은 언제 떠날 거니?　　　　　　　　　　　_____ _____ they going to leave?

8 그녀는 어디 가는 중이니?　　　　　　　　　　_____ _____ she going?

> **WRITING POINT 2**
> • **When do** you go to school? 언제 / 너는 / 가니 / 학교에?
> • **Where does** your mother work? 어디에서 / 네 어머니는 / 일하시니?

I 너는 언제 자러 가니?　　　　　　　　　　　　_____ _____ you go to bed?

2 그는 언제 테니스를 연습하니?　　　　　　　　_____ _____ he practice tennis?

3 너는 어디에서 옷을 사니?　　　　　　　　　　_____ _____ you buy your clothes?

4 그녀는 일요일마다 어디에 가니?　　　　　　　_____ _____ she go on Sundays?

5 너는 언제 그녀를 만났니?　　　　　　　　　　_____ _____ you meet her?

6 그녀는 언제 너에게 전화했니?　　　　　　　　_____ _____ she call you?

7 너는 네 가방을 어디에서 찾았니?　　　　　　　_____ _____ you find your bag?

8 그는 그의 우산을 어디에 두고 왔니?　　　　　_____ _____ he leave his umbrella?

우리말과 일치하도록 빈칸에 알맞은 말을 넣으시오.

• When/Where + be동사 •

1 Jack은 지금 어디 있니?

→ _____ _____ _____ at the moment?

2 미국은 어머니의 날이 언제니? (Mother's Day)

→ _____ _____ _____ _____ in America?

3 네 영어 선생님은 어디 출신이시니? (your English teacher)

→ _____ _____ _____ _____ _____ from?

4 너는 학교 끝나고 어디에 있었니? (you)

→ _____ _____ _____ after school?

5 너는 언제 숙제할거니? (going to)

→ _____ _____ _____ _____ _____ do your homework?

• When/Where + 일반동사 •

6 당신은 주로 어디로 쇼핑하러 가나요? (go shopping)

→ _____ _____ _____ usually _____ _____ ?

7 영화는 언제 시작하니? (start)

→ _____ _____ the movie _____ ?

8 다음 버스는 언제 도착하나요? (arrive)

→ _____ _____ the next bus _____ ?

9 너는 유럽에서 어디를 방문했니? (visit)

→ _____ _____ _____ _____ in Europe?

10 너는 네 선글라스를 언제 잃어버렸니? (lose)

→ _____ _____ _____ _____ your sunglasses?

( ) 안의 말을 이용하여 우리말을 영어로 옮기시오.

1 그의 고향은 어디니? (his hometown)

2 너희 부모님은 어디에 계시니? (your parents)

3 네 집들이는 언제니? (your housewarming party)

4 코알라들은 어디에 사나요? (koalas)

5 백화점은 언제 문을 여나요? (the department store)

6 가장 가까운 버스 정류장이 어디죠? (the nearest bus stop)

7 너는 언제 일본을 여행했니? (travel to)

8 그 사고는 언제 일어난 거죠? (the accident / happen)

9 실종된 아이는 어디에 있었나요? (the missing child)

10 너는 그 드레스를 어디에서 샀니? (the dress)

11 그녀는 태블릿 PC를 언제 잃어버렸니? (her tablet PC)

12 태국은 장마철이 언제 시작되나요? (the rainy season / start / in Thailand)

LESSON 12 who, what

1 의문사 **who**는 '누구'란 뜻으로 **사람**에 대해 물을 때 쓴다.

Who + be동사	Who + be동사 + 주어 ~?	Who *is* he? 그는 누구니?
Who + 일반동사	Who + do/does/did + 주어 + 동사원형 ~?	Who *did* you meet? 너는 누구를 만났니?

PLUS 동사나 전치사의 목적어로 쓰인 의문사 who 대신 whom을 쓸 수도 있다.
e.g. *Who(m)* did you meet? 너는 누구를 만났니?

2 의문사 **what**은 '무엇'이라는 뜻으로 주로 **사물**에 대해 물을 때 쓴다.

What + be동사	What + be동사 + 주어 ~?	What *is* your name? 네 이름은 뭐니?
What + 일반동사	What + do/does/did + 주어 + 동사원형 ~?	What *do* you need? 무엇이 필요하세요?

PLUS 의문사 what은 명사(구)와 결합하여 쓰일 수 있다.
e.g. *What color* is your bag? 네 가방은 무슨 색이니?
What time does the bus leave? 그 버스는 몇 시에 출발하니?

3 의문사 **who**와 **what**은 문장의 **주어**로 쓰일 수 있다. 주어로 쓰인 경우에는 「Who/What+동사 ~?」의 형태로 나타내고, 해석은 각각 '누가', '무엇이'로 한다.

Who + 동사	Who *is* in the garden? 누가 정원에 있니? Who *broke* the window? 누가 창문을 깼니?
What + 동사	What *is* on the table? 탁자 위에 무엇이 있니? What *happened*? 무슨 일이 일어났니?

CHECK UP

● 빈칸에 **Who** 또는 **What**을 쓰시오.

1 A: _____ is the name of your cat?   B: It is Leo.

2 A: _____ was your homeroom teacher?   B: Mr. Wade.

3 A: _____ knows the answer?   B: I know.

4 A: _____ size do you wear?   B: I wear 7.

5 A: _____ do you usually eat for breakfast?   B: Eggs and toast.

6 A: _____ is she?   B: She is my sister, Cathy.

7 A: _____ are you doing?   B: I'm cooking pasta.

8 A: _____ is in the bathroom?   B: Dad.

62

box 안의 예문을 참고하여 우리말과 일치하도록 문장을 완성하시오.

WRITING POINT ①

- **Who are** they? 누구니 / 그들은?
- **What is** her phone number? 무엇이니 / 그녀의 전화번호가?

---

1 저 소녀는 누구니? _____ _____ that girl?

2 너의 가장 친한 친구들이 누구니? _____ _____ your best friends?

3 당신의 주소가 어떻게 되세요? _____ _____ your address?

4 당신의 첫 직업이 무엇이었나요? _____ _____ your first job?

5 그의 차는 무슨 색이니? _____ _____ _____ his car?

WRITING POINT ②

- **Who did** he fight with? 누구와 / 그는 싸웠니?
- **What does** she do after school? 무엇을 / 그녀는 하니 / 방과 후에?

---

1 너는 누구와 함께 일하니? _____ _____ you work with?

2 그녀는 주말에 뭘 하니? _____ _____ she do on the weekend?

3 그들은 누구와 함께 갔니? _____ _____ they go with?

4 너는 쇼핑몰에서 무엇을 샀니? _____ _____ you buy at the mall?

WRITING POINT ③

- **Who is cooking** dinner? 누가 / 요리 중이니 / 저녁을?
- **What happened** this morning? 무슨 일이 / 일어났니 / 오늘 아침에?

---

1 누가 TV를 보고 있니? _____ _____ _____ TV?

2 상자 안에 무엇이 있니? _____ _____ in the box?

3 누가 그 방을 청소했니? _____ _____ the room?

4 그에게 무슨 일이 일어났니? _____ _____ to him?

우리말과 일치하도록 빈칸에 알맞은 말을 넣으시오.

• Who/What + be동사 •

1   사진 속에 있는 사람들은 누구니? (the people)

→ _____ _____ _____ _____ in the picture?

2   너에게 무슨 문제가 있니? (the matter)

→ _____ _____ _____ _____ with you?

3   너는 대학 때 전공이 무엇이었니? (your major)

→ _____ _____ _____ _____ in college?

• Who/What + 일반동사 •

4   네가 가장 좋아하는 사람이 누구니? (like)

→ _____ _____ _____ _____ the most?

5   그는 파티에 누구를 초대했니? (invite)

→ _____ _____ _____ _____ to the party?

6   이 단어는 무슨 뜻이니? (mean)

→ _____ _____ this word _____?

7   너는 보통 몇 시에 자러 가니? (time)

→ _____ _____ _____ _____ usually go to bed?

• Who/What : 주어 •

8   누가 소파에 앉아 있니? (sit)

→ _____ _____ _____ on the sofa?

9   누가 어제 그의 지갑을 훔쳤니? (steal / his wallet)

→ _____ _____ _____ _____ yesterday?

10   무엇이 탁자에서 떨어졌니? (fall off)

→ _____ _____ _____ the table?

( ) 안의 말을 이용하여 우리말을 영어로 옮기시오.

1 누가 너의 쌍둥이 여동생이니? (twin sister)

2 부엌에 누가 있니? (in the kitchen)

3 누가 이 샌드위치들을 만들었니? (these sandwiches)

4 당신의 가장 큰 실수는 무엇이었나요? (your biggest mistake)

5 누가 알람을 껐니? (turn off / the alarm)

6 너는 보통 여가 시간에 뭘 하니? (usually / in your free time)

7 당신은 누구를 가장 존경합니까? (respect / the most)

8 너희 학교는 몇 시에 시작하니? (your school / start)

9 너는 생일 선물로 뭘 원하니? (want / for your birthday)

10 누가 컴퓨터를 사용하고 있니? (use / the computer)

11 네 여자친구는 무엇이 그렇게 특별해? (so special / about your girlfriend)

12 그 사진에서 무엇이 흥미로워 보였어요? (look interesting / in the picture)

LESSON 13
why, how

1 의문사 **why**는 '왜'라는 뜻으로 **이유**를 물을 때 쓴다.

Why + be동사	Why + be동사 + 주어 ~?	Why *are* you so upset? 너는 왜 그렇게 화났니?
Why + 일반동사	Why + do/does/did + 주어 + 동사원형 ~?	Why *do* you like the book? 너는 왜 그 책을 좋아하니?

2 의문사 **how**은 '어떤, 어떻게'라는 뜻으로 **상태**나 **방법**을 물을 때 쓴다.

How + be동사	How + be동사 + 주어 ~?	How *is* the weather today? 오늘 날씨 어때?
How + 일반동사	How + do/does/did + 주어 + 동사원형 ~?	How *does* he get to work? 그는 어떻게 출근하니?

3 의문사 **how**는 다른 **형용사**나 **부사** 앞에 쓰여 '얼마나'란 뜻으로 쓰인다.

How old are you? 너는 몇 살이니?

How far is the library? 도서관은 얼마나 먼가요?

How often do you exercise? 너는 얼마나 자주 운동을 하니?

PLUS '(수가) 얼마나 많은 ~?'이라고 물을 때는 「How many + 복수명사 ~?」로 묻는다.
e.g. *How many people* did you invite to the party? 너는 파티에 몇 명을 초대했니?

● 빈칸에 **Why** 또는 **How**를 쓰시오.

1 A: _____ are you wearing a coat? B: Because it's cold.

2 A: _____ was the movie? B: It was boring.

3 A: _____ is he so happy? B: He got an A in math.

4 A: _____ do you want to be a pilot? B: Because I like flying.

5 A: _____ is your family? B: They are doing fine.

6 A: _____ were you so late? B: I missed the school bus.

7 A: _____ did they go to Jeonju? B: By train.

8 A: _____ did you stay home? B: Because I didn't feel well.

9 A: _____ many books did you read last year? B: About twenty.

10 A: _____ old is your brother? B: He's sixteen.

box 안의 예문을 참고하여 우리말과 일치하도록 문장을 완성하시오.

WRITING POINT ❶

- **Why is** he so popular? 왜 / 그는 그렇게 인기 있니?
- **How are** your parents? 어떠시니 / 네 부모님은?

I 그녀는 왜 그렇게 기분이 좋니? _____ _____ she so happy?

2 그 아이들은 왜 웃고 있니? _____ _____ the children laughing?

3 오늘 어때? _____ _____ you today?

4 너는 왜 수업에 늦었니? _____ _____ you late for class?

5 크리스마스는 어땠니? _____ _____ your Christmas?

WRITING POINT ❷

- **Why do** you learn English? 왜 / 너는 배우니 / 영어를?
- **How did** you get to the airport? 어떻게 / 너는 갔니 / 공항까지?

I 그는 왜 한국을 좋아하니? _____ _____ he like Korea?

2 너는 나한테 왜 전화했니? _____ _____ you call me?

3 그들은 어떻게 여행하니? _____ _____ they travel?

4 그들은 서로 어떻게 만났니? _____ _____ they meet each other?

WRITING POINT ❸

- **How long** is your summer vacation? 얼마나 긴가요 / 당신의 여름 방학은?
- **How many people** came to the party? 얼마나 많은 사람들이 / 왔니 / 파티에?

I 네 남동생은 몇 살이니? _____ _____ is your brother?

2 지하철역은 얼마나 먼가요? _____ _____ is the subway station?

3 너는 얼마나 자주 머리를 감니? _____ _____ do you wash your hair?

4 그는 얼마나 많은 질문을 했니? _____ _____ _____ did he ask?

우리말과 일치하도록 빈칸에 알맞은 말을 넣으시오.

• Why/How + be동사 •

1 런던의 날씨는 어떠니? (the weather)

→ _____ _____ _____ _____ in London?

2 그는 회의에 왜 늦었니? (late)

→ _____ _____ _____ _____ for the meeting?

3 스페인 여행은 어땠니? (your trip)

→ _____ _____ _____ _____ to Spain?

• Why/How + 일반동사 •

4 이 기계는 어떻게 작동하니? (work)

→ _____ _____ this machine _____?

5 그는 왜 항상 불평하니? (complain)

→ _____ _____ _____ always _____?

6 너는 그의 이름을 어떻게 아니? (know)

→ _____ _____ _____ _____ his name?

• How + 형용사/부사 •

7 그의 아들은 몇 살이니?

→ _____ _____ _____ his son?

8 너는 조부모님을 얼마나 자주 찾아 뵙니? (visit)

→ _____ _____ _____ _____ your grandparents?

9 너는 한 달에 외식을 몇 번 하니? (times)

→ _____ _____ _____ _____ _____ eat out a month?

10 너희 학교는 여기서 얼마나 머니? (far)

→ _____ _____ _____ your school from here?

( ) 안의 말을 이용하여 우리말을 영어로 옮기시오.

1 당신 나라의 날씨는 어떻습니까? (in your country)

2 네 수학 시험은 어땠니? (your math test)

3 너는 왜 여름을 좋아하니? (summer)

4 네 아버지는 왜 어제 화가 나셨니? (upset)

5 당신 이름의 철자가 어떻게 되죠? (you / spell)

6 당신은 오늘 아침 어떻게 출근했어요? (get to work)

7 너는 왜 이렇게 서두르니? (in a hurry)

8 그녀는 왜 울고 있니? (crying)

9 표가 몇 장이나 필요하세요? (tickets / need)

10 너는 얼마나 자주 이를 닦니? (brush your teeth)

11 그는 왜 그의 직장을 그만두었니? (quit / his job)

12 너는 몇 번이나 그녀에게 데이트 신청을 했니? (times / ask her out)

1 다음 대화의 빈칸에 알맞은 의문사를 쓰시오.

(1) **A** _____ is your best friend?

B My best friend is Susie.

(2) **A** _____ is Minsu?

B He is in the classroom.

(3) **A** _____ _____ do you play tennis?

B I play tennis twice a week.

2 (A)와 (B)에서 각각 한 표현씩을 골라 질문을 완성하시오.

(A)	(B)
What	are you from?
When	is your name?
Where	is your birthday?

(1) _____

(2) _____

(3) _____

3 주어진 단어를 바르게 배열하여 문장을 완성하시오.

(1) (did / when / he / friends / meet / his)

→ _____

(2) (usually / you / time / get up / do / what)

→ _____

4 우리말과 같은 뜻이 되도록 주어진 단어를 바르게 배열하시오.

당신은 몇 명의 형제 자매가 있나요?
(sisters / many / and / you / how / do / have / brothers)

→ _____

5 그림을 보고 주어진 단어를 이용하여 A의 질문을 완성하시오.

A _____ _____ _____ last night? (what, do)

B I watched TV.

6 다음 대화의 빈칸에 들어갈 질문을 〈조건〉에 맞게 완성하시오.

> 조건 1. 주어와 동사를 갖춘 완전한 문장으로 쓸 것
>   2. 주어진 단어를 이용할 것

A (1) _____
(favorite teacher)

B I like Mr. Kim.

A (2) _____
(subject, teach)

B He teaches music.

(1) _____

(2) _____

7 주어진 정보를 보고 다음 대화를 완성하시오.

Movie Party Invitation	
Title	*Beauty and the Beast*
When	Sat. July 10th, 6-8 p.m.
Where	Joan's House

A (1) _____ _____ _____ of the movie?

B It's *Beauty and the Beast*.

A (2) _____ _____ it _____ _____ ?

B It takes place at Joan's house.

UNIT
06

문장의 형식

LESSON 14 · There is/are, 비인칭 주어 it

1 There is/are는 '~(들)이 있다'란 뜻이다. 여기서 there는 특별한 의미가 없으므로 '거기에'라고 해석하지 않는다. There is 뒤에는 **단수명사**, There are 뒤에는 **복수명사**가 온다.

긍정문	There is + 단수명사 There are + 복수명사	There is *a car* in the garage. 차고에 차가 한 대 있다. There are *books* on the bookshelf. 책장에 책들이 있다.
부정문	There is/are + not	There is not[isn't] *a car* in the garage. 차고에 차가 없다.
의문문	Is/Are there ~?	A: Are there *books* on the bookshelf? 책장에 책들이 있니? B: Yes, there are. / No, there aren't. 응, 있어. / 아니, 없어.

PLUS '~(들)이 있었다'는 「There was + 단수명사」 또는 「There were + 복수명사」를 쓴다.

> e.g. *There was* a car in the garage. 차고에 차가 한 대 있었다.
> *There were* books on the bookshelf. 책장에 책들이 있었다.

2 비인칭 주어 it은 날씨, 시간, 요일, 날짜, 거리, 명암 등을 나타내는 문장의 주어로 쓰인다. 이때 it은 형식적인 주어이므로 '그것'이라고 해석하지 않는다.

날씨	A: How is the weather today? 오늘 날씨가 어떠니?	B: It's sunny. 화창해.
시간	A: What time is it now? 지금 몇 시니?	B: It's 4 o'clock. 4시야.
요일, 날짜	A: What day is it? 무슨 요일이니? A: What date is it? 며칠이니?	B: It's Wednesday. 수요일이야. B: It's April 5th. 4월 5일이야.
거리, 명암	It takes 10 minutes from here. 여기서 10분 걸려. It is dark outside. 밖이 어둡다.	

CHECK UP

● 빈칸에 알맞은 말을 고르시오.

1 _____ is a clock on the wall. ☐ There ☐ It

2 _____ is Friday today. ☐ There ☐ It

3 _____ aren't any clouds in the sky. ☐ There ☐ It

4 _____ is snowing a lot. ☐ There ☐ It

5 _____ is some milk in the fridge. ☐ There ☐ It

6 Is _____ a supermarket near here? ☐ there ☐ it

7 _____ is 3 kilometers from here. ☐ There ☐ It

8 _____ isn't any water in the bottle. ☐ There ☐ It

box 안의 예문을 참고하여 우리말과 일치하도록 문장을 완성하시오.

WRITING POINT ①

- **There is** a TV in the living room. 있다 / TV가 / 거실에
- **There isn't** a TV in the living room. 없다 / TV가 / 거실에
- **Is there** a TV in the living room? 있니 / TV가 / 거실에?

I 이 방에는 창문이 있다. _____ _____ a window in this room.

2 이 방에는 창문이 없다. _____ _____ a window in this room.

3 도로에 차들이 많이 있다. _____ _____ many cars on the road.

4 도로에 차들이 많이 없다. _____ _____ many cars on the road.

5 이 근처에 은행이 있다. _____ _____ a bank near here.

6 이 근처에 은행이 있니? _____ _____ a bank near here?

7 공원에 아이들이 있다. _____ _____ children in the park.

8 공원에 아이들이 있니? _____ _____ children in the park?

WRITING POINT ②

- **It is** very hot today. (날씨가) 매우 덥다 / 오늘은

I 밖에 비가 오고 있다. _____ _____ raining outside.

2 오늘은 춥지 않다. _____ _____ cold today.

3 거의 7시다. _____ _____ nearly seven o'clock.

4 8월 1일이다. _____ _____ August 1st.

5 오늘은 내 생일이다. _____ _____ my birthday today.

6 여기서 멀지 않다. _____ _____ far from here.

7 이 안은 매우 어둡다. _____ _____ very dark in here.

8 지금 몇 시니? What time _____ _____ now?

9 오늘이 무슨 요일이니? What day _____ _____ today?

우리말과 일치하도록 빈칸에 알맞은 말을 넣으시오.

• There is/are •

1   정원에 큰 나무 한 그루가 있다. (a big tree)

→ _____ _____ _____ _____ _____ in the garden.

2   우리 반에는 30명의 학생들이 있다. (thirty students)

→ _____ _____ _____ _____ in our class.

3   유리잔에 물이 전혀 없다. (any water)

→ _____ _____ _____ _____ in the glass.

4   이 근처에 주차장이 있나요? (a parking lot)

→ _____ _____ _____ _____ _____ near here?

5   식구가 몇 명이나 되나요? (people)

→ How many _____ _____ _____ in your family?

• 비인칭 주어 it •

6   여름에는 비가 많이 온다. (rain / a lot)

→ _____ _____ _____ _____ in summer.

7   이 안은 매우 덥다. (very hot)

→ _____ _____ _____ _____ in here.

8   오늘이 며칠이니? (date)

→ What _____ _____ _____ today?

9   어제는 스승의 날이었다. (Teacher's Day)

→ _____ _____ _____ _____ yesterday.

10   여기서 공항까지는 10킬로미터이다. (10 kilometers)

→ _____ _____ _____ _____ to the airport from here.

( ) 안의 말을 이용하여 우리말을 영어로 옮기시오.

1   언덕 위에 집 한 채가 있다. (on the top of the hill)

2   밖에 비가 오고 있니? (it / outside)

3   어제는 따뜻하고 화창했다. (it / warm / sunny)

4   1년에는 사계절이 있다. (seasons / in a year)

5   저에게 온 우편물이 있나요? (any mail / for me)

6   이제 겨우 10시다. (it / only)

7   오늘은 크리스마스야! (it / Christmas)

8   이 근처에 괜찮은 음식점이 있니? (any good restaurants)

9   그 정원에는 꽃이 많지 않다. (many flowers)

10   11월 15일이다. (November 15th)

11   오늘 저녁에 공원에서 콘서트가 있다. (a concert / in the park)

12   자전거로 10분 걸려요. (take / 10 minutes / by bike)

감각동사 + 형용사

1 감각동사는 다섯 가지 감각을 나타내는 동사로 **look**, **feel**, **sound**, **smell**, **taste**가 있다. 이 동사들은 「**감각동사＋형용사**」 형태로 쓰여 '~하게 보이다/느껴지다/들리다/냄새가 나다/맛이 나다'의 의미로 쓰인다.

You **look** *happy*. 너는 행복해 보인다.
This fur **feels** *soft*. 이 털은 부드럽게 느껴진다.
It **sounds** *great*. 그것은 매우 좋게 들린다.
It **smells** *delicious*. 그것은 맛있는 냄새가 난다.
This orange **tastes** *sour*. 이 오렌지는 신맛이 난다.

2 감각동사 뒤에 「**like＋명사**」가 오면 '~처럼 보이다/느껴지다/들리다/냄새가 나다/맛이 나다'란 뜻이다. 전치사 like 뒤에는 반드시 **명사**를 써야 한다.

She **looks like** *an angel*. 그녀는 천사처럼 보인다.
It **feels like** *home*. 그곳은 집처럼 느껴진다.
It **sounds like** *a good idea*. 그거 좋은 생각 같구나.
It **smells like** *fish*. 그것은 생선 같은 냄새가 난다.
They **taste like** *my mom's cooking*. 그것들은 나의 엄마가 해주신 요리 같은 맛이 난다.

CHECK UP

● 빈칸에 알맞은 말을 고르시오.

1	This sweater _____ very soft.	☐ feels	☐ feels like
2	Terry _____ a nice person.	☐ looks	☐ looks like
3	His voice _____ lovely to me.	☐ sounds	☐ sounds like
4	This book doesn't _____ interesting.	☐ look	☐ look like
5	Kevin _____ sick all day.	☐ felt	☐ felt like
6	I _____ a movie star.	☐ feel	☐ feel like
7	Linda _____ her sister.	☐ looks	☐ looks like
8	My coffee _____ bitter.	☐ tastes	☐ tastes like
9	This soap _____ a lemon.	☐ smells	☐ smells like
10	She's old but she still _____ beautiful.	☐ looks	☐ looks like

box 안의 예문을 참고하여 우리말과 일치하도록 문장을 완성하시오.

WRITING POINT ①

· You **look tired** today. 너는 / 피곤해 보인다 / 오늘

---

1 그것들은 모두 다르게 생겼다.　　　　They all _____ _____.

2 이 담요는 따뜻하게 느껴진다.　　　　This blanket _____ _____.

3 그녀의 목소리는 아름답게 들린다.　　Her voice _____ _____.

4 이 과일 차는 달콤한 맛이 난다.　　　This fruit tea _____ _____.

5 그 쿠키들은 맛있는 냄새가 난다.　　　The cookies _____ _____.

6 그의 개는 매우 똑똑해 보인다.　　　　His dog _____ very _____.

7 그 채소들은 신선해 보이지 않는다.　　The vegetables _____ _____ _____.

8 그 피아노는 소리가 좋지 않다.　　　　The piano _____ _____ _____.

9 그것은 맛이 좋으니?　　　　　　　　Does it _____ _____?

WRITING POINT ②

· The robot **looks like** a human. 그 로봇은 / 보인다 / 사람처럼

---

1 이 그림은 사진처럼 보인다.　　　　　This picture _____ _____ a photo.

2 이 블라우스는 실크처럼 느껴진다.　　This blouse _____ _____ silk.

3 그것은 좋은 계획처럼 들린다.　　　　It _____ _____ a good plan.

4 그것은 인도 음식 같은 냄새가 난다.　It _____ _____ Indian food.

5 이 고기는 닭고기 같은 맛이 난다.　　This meat _____ _____ chicken.

6 미나는 그녀의 엄마를 닮았다.　　　　Mina _____ _____ her mother.

7 그들은 서로 닮지 않았다.　　　　　　They _____ _____ _____ each other.

8 그것은 좋은 생각처럼 들리지 않는다.　That _____ _____ a good idea.

9 그는 어떻게 생겼어?　　　　　　　　What does he _____ _____?

우리말과 일치하도록 빈칸에 알맞은 말을 넣으시오.

• 감각동사 + 형용사 •

1 너는 그 드레스를 입으니 예뻐 보인다. (lovely)

→ You _____ _____ in that dress.

2 이 약은 맛이 쓰다. (bitter)

→ This medicine _____ _____.

3 이 소파는 편안하게 느껴진다. (comfortable)

→ This sofa _____ _____.

4 그 플루트는 소리가 아름답다. (beautiful)

→ The flute _____ _____.

5 이 방에서 이상한 냄새가 난다. (weird)

→ This room _____ _____.

• 감각동사 + like + 명사 •

6 그는 좋은 선생님처럼 보인다. (a good teacher)

→ He _____ _____ _____ _____ _____.

7 이 샴푸는 장미 냄새가 난다. (roses)

→ This shampoo _____ _____ _____.

8 그것은 흥미로운 주제처럼 들린다. (an interesting topic)

→ It _____ _____ _____ _____.

9 이 아이스크림은 녹차 맛이 난다. (green tea)

→ This ice cream _____ _____ _____ _____.

10 이 베개는 돌처럼 느껴진다. (a stone)

→ This pillow _____ _____ _____ _____.

( ) 안의 말을 이용하여 우리말을 영어로 옮기시오.

I 그것은 농담처럼 들린다. (that / a joke)

2 이 노래는 친숙하게 들린다. (familiar)

3 그 영화배우는 그리스 조각상처럼 보인다. (the movie star / a Greek statue)

4 그의 설명은 어렵게 들린다. (his explanation / difficult)

5 이 손수건은 촉감이 부드럽다. (handkerchief / soft)

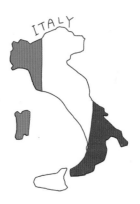

6 이탈리아 지도는 부츠처럼 보인다. (the map of Italy / a boot)

7 이 사진 속의 사람들은 행복해 보인다. (the people in this picture)

8 이 향수는 좋은 냄새가 난다. (this perfume / nice)

9 나는 네가 없으면 외롭게 느껴져. (lonely / without you)

10 나는 가끔 천재처럼 느껴진다. (sometimes / a genius)

11 Dave는 연설하기 전에 초조함을 느꼈다. (nervous / before the speech)

12 그 과일은 딸기처럼 보이지만 파인애플 같은 맛이 난다. (a strawberry / a pineapple)

수여동사

I 수여동사는 「주어＋동사＋간접목적어(사람)＋직접목적어(사물)」 형태로 쓰여 '간접목적어에게 직접목적어를 ~하다'란 의미를 갖는다.

Joe **gave** <u>me</u> <u>a nice present</u>. Joe는 나에게 멋진 선물을 주었다.
간·목   직·목

Dad will **cook** <u>us</u> <u>dinner</u> tonight. 아빠는 오늘 밤 우리에게 저녁을 요리해주실 것이다.
간·목 직·목

2 수여동사가 쓰인 문장은 간접목적어와 직접목적어의 위치를 바꾸어 쓸 수 있다. 이때 **간접목적어** 앞에 **전치사(to, for, of 등)**를 써야 한다.

to를 쓰는 동사	give(주다), lend(빌려주다), send(보내다), show(보여주다), tell(말하다), write(쓰다), teach(가르치다) 등	Sally sent me a postcard. → Sally sent a postcard to me. Sally는 나에게 엽서 한 장을 보냈다.
for를 쓰는 동사	buy(사다), make(만들다), cook(요리하다), bring(가져오다), find(찾다) 등	Tom bought Jane some flowers. → Tom bought some flowers for Jane. Tom은 Jane에게 꽃을 사주었다.
of를 쓰는 동사	ask(묻다)	I asked him a question. → I asked a question of him. 나는 그에게 질문을 하나 했다.

CHECK UP

- 간접목적어에는 동그라미를 하고, 직접목적어에는 밑줄을 치시오.

1 Ryan gave me a box of candy.

2 I will lend you my notebook.

3 Mary made her daughter a pretty doll.

4 Jim told us his plans.

5 He asked me a lot of questions.

6 John showed me his new cell phone.

7 Jessica sent her friend an email.

8 She teaches her kids English.

9 Jane's mother bought her a dress.

10 May I ask you some questions?

box 안의 예문을 참고하여 우리말과 일치하도록 문장을 완성하시오.

WRITING POINT ①

• My grandma <u>**sent me**</u> a present. 나의 할머니는 / 보내셨다 / 나에게 / 선물 하나를

1 그들은 우리에게 팩스 한 장을 보냈다. They _____ _____ a fax.

2 나는 Mike에게 이메일을 썼다. I _____ _____ an email.

3 그는 나에게 사진 한 장을 보여주었다. He _____ _____ a picture.

4 Karen은 나에게 비밀 하나를 말해주었다. Karen _____ _____ a secret.

5 나는 Jane에게 내 카메라를 빌려주었다. I _____ _____ my camera.

6 김 선생님은 우리에게 수학을 가르치신다. Mr. Kim _____ _____ math.

7 나는 내 여동생에게 책 한 권을 사주었다. I _____ _____ _____ a book.

8 그는 우리에게 피자를 만들어주었다. He _____ _____ pizza.

9 그는 나에게 질문을 하나 했다. He _____ _____ a question.

WRITING POINT ②

• My grandma sent a present **to me**. 나의 할머니는 / 보내셨다 / 선물 하나를 / 나에게

1 그들은 우리에게 팩스 한 장을 보냈다. They sent a fax _____ _____ .

2 나는 Mike에게 이메일을 썼다. I wrote an email _____ _____ .

3 그는 나에게 사진 한 장을 보여주었다. He showed a picture _____ _____ .

4 Karen은 나에게 비밀 하나를 말해주었다. Karen told a secret _____ _____ .

5 나는 Jane에게 내 카메라를 빌려주었다. I lent my camera _____ _____ .

6 김 선생님은 우리에게 수학을 가르치신다. Mr. Kim teaches math _____ _____ .

7 나는 내 여동생에게 책 한 권을 사주었다. I bought a book _____ _____ _____ .

8 그는 우리에게 피자를 만들어주었다. He made pizza _____ _____ .

9 그는 나에게 질문을 하나 했다. He asked a question _____ _____ .

SENTENCE PRACTICE 2

우리말과 일치하도록 빈칸에 알맞은 말을 넣으시오.

• 주어 + 동사 + 간·목 + 직·목 •

1 그는 나에게 그의 노트를 빌려주었다. (his notebook)

→ He _____ _____ _____ _____.

2 너는 Mary에게 소포를 보냈니? (the parcel)

→ Did you _____ _____ _____ _____?

3 나는 나의 선생님에게 감사 편지를 썼다. (a thank-you letter)

→ I _____ _____ _____ _____ _____ _____.

4 물 한 잔만 갖다 줄래요? (a glass of water)

→ Can you _____ _____ _____ _____ _____ _____?

5 수업 중에 너는 나에게 어떤 질문도 할 수 있다. (any questions)

→ You can _____ _____ _____ _____ during the class.

• 주어 + 동사 + 직·목 + 전치사 + 간·목 •

6 나는 내 남동생에게 장난감 자동차를 사주었다. (a toy car)

→ I _____ _____ _____ _____ my brother.

7 필요하면 내가 천원을 빌려줄게. (1,000 won)

→ I will _____ _____ _____ _____ you if you need.

8 엄마는 나에게 커다란 케이크를 만들어주었다. (a huge cake)

→ My mom _____ _____ _____ _____ _____ me.

9 Lucy는 그녀의 그림을 자신의 반 친구들에게 보여주었다. (her painting)

→ Lucy _____ _____ _____ _____ her classmates.

10 그들은 항상 서로에게 진실을 말한다. (the truth)

→ They always _____ _____ _____ _____ each other.

( ) 안의 말을 이용하여 우리말을 영어로 옮기시오.

1 Frank는 우리에게 재미있는 이야기를 하나 해주었다. (a funny story)

2 넌 나에게 거짓말을 하면 안 돼. (should / a lie)

3 그 여행은 나에게 특별한 경험을 주었다. (the trip / a special experience)

4 나의 삼촌은 내 생일에 나에게 선물을 보내주었다. (a present / on my birthday)

5 아빠는 일주일에 한 번 우리에게 저녁을 요리해주신다. (once a week)

6 Linda는 나에게 멋진 모자를 만들어주었다. (a nice hat)

7 Steve는 그의 차를 누구에게도 빌려주지 않는다. (lend / anyone)

8 Mindy는 나에게 한자를 몇 자 가르쳐주었다. (some Chinese characters)

9 그는 그의 딸에게 강아지 한 마리를 사 주었다. (his daughter / a puppy)

10 그 기자들은 그 소녀에게 많은 질문을 했다. (the reporters / a lot of questions)

11 그 책은 나에게 많은 교훈들을 가르쳐주었다. (a lot of lessons)

12 그는 우리에게 그의 정원에서 수확한 채소들을 주었다. (the vegetables from his garden)

I 다음 질문에 알맞은 답을 쓰시오.

A How is the weather today?
B _____ _____ rainy.

2 주어진 단어를 이용하여 다음 대화의 밑줄 친 우리말을 영작하시오.

A How far is it from here to the station?
B 걸어서 5분 걸려. (take, minute, on foot)

→ _____

3 그림을 보고 주어진 단어를 이용하여 빈칸에 알맞은 말을 쓰시오.

(1) There _____ _____ _____ on the sofa. (dog)
(2) There _____ _____ _____ on the table. (two)
(3) There _____ _____ _____ on the wall. (picture)

4 각 문장의 빈칸에 적절한 단어를 〈보기〉에서 한 번씩만 사용하여 문장을 완성하시오. (단, 필요하면 어법에 맞는 형태로 바꾸어 쓸 것)

보기   look / feel / taste

(1) This rug _____ soft.
(2) This cake _____ sweet.
(3) You _____ serious today.

5 주어진 단어를 이용하여 우리말을 영작하시오.

(1) 그의 목소리는 친근하게 들린다. (friendly)

→ _____

(2) 그것은 좋은 생각처럼 들린다. (it, a good idea)

→ _____

6 주어진 단어를 바르게 배열하여 문장을 완성하시오.

(1) (her family / sent / she / her pictures)

→ _____

(2) (delicious / my dad / I / make / will / cookies)

→ _____

7 두 문장이 같은 의미가 되도록 빈칸에 알맞은 말을 쓰시오.

(1) My friend lent me an interesting book.

= My friend _____ _____ _____ _____ _____.

(2) I bought my sister a hairpin.

= I bought _____ _____ _____ _____ _____.

UNIT
07

to부정사와 동명사

LESSON 17 to부정사의 명사적 용법

1 「to+동사원형」인 to부정사는 문장에서 명사가 하는 역할인 **주어, 보어, 목적어** 역할을 할 수 있고, '~하는 것'으로 해석한다.

주어 역할 (~하는 것은)	to부정사 + 단수동사	To study *is* important. 공부하는 것은 중요하다.
보어 역할 (~하는 것이다)	be동사 + to부정사	My plan *is* to study. 내 계획은 공부하는 것이다.
목적어 역할 (~하는 것을)	동사 + to부정사	I *want* to study. 나는 공부하는 것을 원한다.

NOTE to부정사를 목적어로 취하는 동사

> want(원하다), like(좋아하다), hope(바라다), wish(바라다), plan(계획하다), decide(결심하다), need(필요하다), try(노력하다), learn(배우다), promise(약속하다) 등

> e.g. I need *to send* him an email. 나는 그에게 이메일을 보내야 한다.
> He decided *to join* the drama club. 그는 연극 반에 가입하기로 결심했다.

2 주어로 쓰인 to부정사구가 길 때 **가주어 it**을 쓰고 to부정사구는 문장 뒤로 보낼 수 있다. 이때 it은 형식적인 주어이므로 '그것'이라고 해석하지 않는다.

To eat a lot of junk food is not healthy. 정크푸드를 많이 먹는 것은 건강에 좋지 않다.

→ **It** is not healthy **to eat a lot of junk food**.
　　가주어　　　　　　　　　　　　진주어

CHECK UP

● 밑줄 친 부분의 알맞은 뜻을 고르시오.

1 I hope to see you soon. ☐ 만나는 것은 ☐ 만나는 것을

2 To learn to swim is always fun. ☐ 배우는 것은 ☐ 배우는 것을

3 Jack promised to come again. ☐ 오는 것은 ☐ 오는 것을

4 My dream is to be a pilot. ☐ 되는 것(이다) ☐ 되는 것을

5 Aron wants to buy a new car. ☐ 사는 것(이다) ☐ 사는 것을

6 To help each other is important. ☐ 돕는 것은 ☐ 돕는 것(이다)

7 I like to travel by train. ☐ 여행하는 것(이다) ☐ 여행하는 것을

8 His plan is to study abroad. ☐ 공부하는 것(이다) ☐ 공부하는 것을

9 To win the race is their goal. ☐ 이기는 것은 ☐ 이기는 것(이다)

box 안의 예문을 참고하여 우리말과 일치하도록 문장을 완성하시오.

WRITING POINT ❶

• **It** is useful **to learn** a foreign language. 유용하다 / 외국어를 배우는 것은

1	중국어를 배우는 것은 어렵다.	It is difficult _____ Chinese.
2	캠핑을 가는 것은 재미있다.	It is fun _____ camping.
3	자전거를 타는 것은 재미있다.	It is fun _____ a bicycle.
4	다른 사람들을 돕는 것은 중요하다.	It is important _____ others.
5	건강에 좋은 음식을 먹는 것은 중요하다.	It is important _____ healthy food.

WRITING POINT ❷

• My plan is **to exercise** regularly. 내 계획은 / 이다 / 규칙적으로 운동하는 것

1	내 계획은 돈을 저축하는 것이다.	My plan is _____ money.
2	내 취미는 소설을 읽는 것이다.	My hobby is _____ novels.
3	내 취미는 음악을 듣는 것이다.	My hobby is _____ to music.
4	내 꿈은 화가가 되는 것이다.	My dream is _____ an artist.
5	내 꿈은 요리사가 되는 것이다.	My dream is _____ a cook.

WRITING POINT ❸

• I want **to travel** around the world. 나는 / 원한다 / 전 세계를 여행하는 것을

1	나는 그 책을 사고 싶다.	I want _____ the book.
2	그들은 집을 청소할 계획이다.	They plan _____ the house.
3	그들은 설거지를 할 계획이다.	They plan _____ the dishes.
4	너는 안경을 쓸 필요가 있다.	You need _____ glasses.
5	너는 그들에게 진실을 말할 필요가 있다.	You need _____ them the truth.

우리말과 일치하도록 빈칸에 알맞은 말을 넣으시오.

• It(가주어) ~ to부정사(진주어) •

1 수학 시험에서 A⁺를 받는 것은 불가능하다. (impossible / get an A⁺)

→ It is _____ _____ _____ _____ _____ on the math exam.

2 서울에 사는 것은 절대 지루하지 않다. (never / boring)

→ It is _____ _____ _____ _____ in Seoul.

3 야채를 먹는 것은 건강에 좋다. (healthy / vegetables)

→ It is _____ _____ _____ .

4 아기를 돌보는 것은 쉽지 않다. (easy / take care of)

→ It is _____ _____ _____ _____ _____ a baby.

• to부정사의 명사적 용법: 보어 •

5 나의 바람은 나의 가족과 하와이에서 사는 것이다. (in Hawaii)

→ My wish is _____ _____ _____ _____ with my family.

6 나의 계획은 방과 후 머리를 자르는 것이다. (get a haircut)

→ My plan is _____ _____ _____ _____ after class.

7 그의 꿈은 대통령이 되는 것이다. (be)

→ His dream is _____ _____ president.

• to부정사의 명사적 용법: 목적어 •

8 Jim과 Sue는 함께 시간 보내기를 원한다. (spend time)

→ Jim and Sue _____ _____ _____ _____ together.

9 Mary는 사진 찍는 것을 좋아한다. (take pictures)

→ Mary _____ _____ _____ _____ .

10 당신은 왜 가수가 되기로 결심했나요? (be)

→ Why did you _____ _____ _____ _____ _____ ?

to부정사와 ( ) 안의 말을 이용하여 우리말을 영어로 옮기시오.

1 아침 6시에 일어나는 것은 쉽지 않다. (it / get up / at 6)

2 그녀는 첼로를 연주하기를 원한다. (the cello)

3 Eric은 공항에 나를 데리러 온다고 약속했다. (promise / pick me up)

4 내 숙제는 나의 특별한 재능에 대해서 글을 쓰는 것이다. (write about / special talent)

5 외국어를 배우는 것은 좋은 생각이다. (it / a foreign language)

6 내 꿈은 우주비행사가 되는 것이다. (become / an astronaut)

7 매일 우유 한 잔을 마시는 것은 좋다. (it / a glass of milk)

8 내 계획은 매일 팔 굽혀 펴기를 하는 것이다. (do push-ups)

9 그 일을 내일까지 끝내는 것은 불가능하다. (impossible / by tomorrow)

10 우리는 이번 주말에 양로원을 방문할 계획이다. (the nursing home)

11 소미(Somi)는 생일 선물로 인형을 받기를 원한다. (get / a doll / for her birthday)

12 그 수학 문제를 푸는 것은 매우 쉬웠다. (it / the math problem)

1 to부정사가 형용사처럼 **명사를 수식**하는 역할을 하는 것을 **to부정사의 형용사적 용법**이라고 한다. 이때 to부정사는 '~하는, ~할'이란 뜻이며, 일반적인 형용사와는 달리 명사를 뒤에서 수식한다.

It is *time* **to go** home. 집에 갈 시간이다.

She needs *someone* **to talk to**. 그녀는 이야기할 누군가가 필요하다.

> **PLUS** -thing/one/body로 끝나는 말이 형용사와 to부정사의 수식을 받을 때는 「-thing/one/body + 형용사 + to부정사」의 어순을 쓴다.
> e.g. I want *something cold to drink*. 나는 시원한 마실 것을 원해.

2 to부정사는 **목적**을 나타내어 '~하기 위해'란 뜻으로도 쓰일 수 있다. 이렇게 목적을 나타내는 것을 **to부정사의 부사적 용법**이라 하며, 문장의 앞과 뒤에 위치할 수 있다.

To learn English, he went to Canada. 영어를 배우기 위해, 그는 캐나다에 갔다.
I got up early **to catch** the first train. 나는 첫 기차를 타기 위해 일찍 일어났다.

CHECK UP

● 밑줄 친 부분의 알맞은 뜻을 고르시오.

1 Do you want something to eat? ☐ 먹을 ☐ 먹기 위해

2 To pass the exam, John studied hard. ☐ 합격할 ☐ 합격하기 위해

3 I need some books to read on the plane. ☐ 읽을 ☐ 읽기 위해

4 There is no chair to sit on. ☐ 앉을 ☐ 앉기 위해

5 They went to the park to fly a kite. ☐ 날릴 ☐ 날리기 위해

6 She studied Japanese to work in Japan. ☐ 일할 ☐ 일하기 위해

7 I didn't have a dress to wear to the wedding. ☐ 입을 ☐ 입기 위해

8 Sean went out to meet his friends. ☐ 만날 ☐ 만나기 위해

9 Do you have a lot of work to do? ☐ 할 ☐ 하기 위해

10 I am writing this email to ask you a question. ☐ 물어볼 ☐ 묻기 위해

box 안의 예문을 참고하여 우리말과 일치하도록 문장을 완성하시오.

WRITING POINT ①

· We don't have much time **to waste**. 우리는 / 없다 / 많은 시간이 / 낭비할

1 그는 할 일이 많이 있다. He has a lot of work _____.

2 나는 쓸 돈이 전혀 없다. I don't have any money _____.

3 너는 나와 이야기할 시간이 있니? Do you have time _____ to me?

4 그 개는 먹을 것을 찾고 있다. The dog is looking for something _____.

5 너는 밤에 입을 재킷이 필요하다. You need a jacket _____ at night.

6 나는 쇼핑하러 갈 시간이 없다. I don't have time _____ shopping.

7 그는 그를 도와줄 친구들이 많다. He has many friends _____ him.

8 한국에는 방문할 곳이 많이 있다. There are many places _____ in Korea.

9 나는 쓸 펜이 하나 필요하다. I need a pen _____ with.

WRITING POINT ②

· People exercise **to stay** healthy. 사람들은 / 운동한다 / 건강을 유지하기 위해

1 나는 공부하기 위해 도서관에 갔다. I went to the library _____.

2 우리는 수영하기 위해 해변에 갔다. We went to the beach _____.

3 그는 새 자전거를 사기 위해 돈을 모았다. He saved money _____ a new bike.

4 나는 엄마를 돕기 위해 집을 청소했다. I cleaned the house _____ my mom.

5 그는 시험에 합격하기 위해 공부 중이다. He is studying _____ the exam.

6 나의 가족은 저녁을 먹기 위해 나갔다. My family went out _____ dinner.

7 그들은 길을 찾기 위해 지도를 보았다. They looked at the map _____ the way.

8 그는 음악을 듣기 위해 라디오를 켰다. He turned on the radio _____ to music.

9 그녀는 에펠탑을 보기 위해 파리에 갔다. She went to Paris _____ the Eiffel Tower.

우리말과 일치하도록 빈칸에 알맞은 말을 넣으시오.

• to부정사의 형용사적 용법 •

1 모든 사람은 사랑할 누군가가 필요하다. (someone)

→ Everyone needs _____ _____ _____.

2 나는 이번 주에 해야 할 숙제가 많다.

→ I have a lot of _____ _____ _____ this week.

3 우리는 이 문제를 해결할 방법을 찾아야 한다. (a way)

→ We have to find _____ _____ _____ _____ this problem.

4 걱정할 것이 없다. (nothing / worry about)

→ There is _____ _____ _____ _____.

5 그들은 살 집을 찾고 있다. (live in)

→ They are looking for _____ _____ _____ _____ _____.

• to부정사의 부사적 용법: 목적 •

6 그는 살을 빼기 위해 매일 아침 조깅을 하러 간다. (lose weight)

→ He goes jogging every morning _____ _____ _____.

7 우리는 일출을 보기 위해 일찍 일어났다. (see / the sunrise)

→ We got up early _____ _____ _____ _____.

8 너에게 그냥 인사하려고 전화했어. (say hello)

→ I just called you _____ _____ _____.

9 나는 이메일을 쓰기 위해 컴퓨터를 켰다. (an email)

→ I turned on the computer _____ _____ _____ _____.

10 Helen은 세계를 여행하기 위해 돈을 저축하고 있다. (travel)

→ Helen is saving money _____ _____ _____ _____.

to부정사와 (   ) 안의 말을 이용하여 우리말을 영어로 옮기시오.

1 나는 개를 산책시키기 위해 공원에 갔다. (walk my dog)

2 점심 먹을 시간이다. (it / have lunch)

3 그 남자는 돌봐야 할 개가 세 마리 있다. (take care of)

4 너는 네 눈을 보호하기 위해 선글라스를 써야 한다. (should / sunglasses / protect)

5 그는 대기오염을 줄이기 위한 방법을 소개했다. (a way / reduce / air pollution)

6 민수(Minsu)는 좋은 성적을 받기 위해 밤새 공부했다. (all night / get good grades)

7 너는 쓸 펜이 있니? (write with)

8 당신은 '아니요'라고 말할 권리가 있다. (the right / say no)

9 그들은 어려움에 처한 사람들을 돕기 위해 돈을 모으고 있다. (collect / people in need)

10 에베레스트 산(Mt. Everest)에 오르기 위해, 그는 네팔(Nepal)로 떠났다. (climb / leave for)

11 그 과학자들은 지구 온난화를 논의하기 위해 회의를 했다. (a meeting / discuss / global warming)

12 Kelly와 Paul은 이야기할 것이 없었다. (nothing / talk about)

동명사는 「동사+-ing」 형태로 문장에서 **명사**처럼 쓰인다. 명사적 용법의 to부정사처럼 **주어, 보어, 목적어** 역할을 할 수 있다.

주어 역할 (~하는 것은)	동명사 + 단수동사	Eating vegetables *is* good for you. 야채를 먹는 것은 너에게 좋다.
보어 역할 (~하는 것이다)	be동사 + 동명사	My hobby *is* playing soccer. 내 취미는 축구 하는 것이다.
목적어 역할 (~하는 것을)	동사 + 동명사, 전치사 + 동명사	I *enjoy* skiing in winter. 나는 겨울에 스키 타는 것을 즐긴다. She is good *at* singing. 그녀는 노래하는 것을 잘한다.

NOTE 동명사를 목적어로 취하는 동사

> enjoy(즐기다), keep(계속하다), finish(끝내다), quit(그만두다), give up(포기하다), mind(꺼리다), avoid(피하다) 등

> e.g. He finished *washing* the dishes. 그는 설거지하는 것을 끝냈다.
> Jiho keeps *coming* late for classes. 지호는 계속해서 수업에 늦게 온다.

to부정사와 동명사를 둘 다 목적어로 취할 수 있는 동사

> like(좋아하다), love(매우 좋아하다), start(시작하다), begin(시작하다), hate(싫어하다) 등

> e.g. Cathy likes *drawing* pictures. Cathy는 그림 그리는 것을 좋아한다.
> = Cathy likes *to draw* pictures.

PLUS 보어로 쓰인 동명사 vs. 현재진행형
동명사는 '~하는 것'이란 뜻으로 명사 역할을 하지만, 현재진행형은 '~하고 있다', '~하는 중이다'란 뜻으로 쓰인다.
> e.g. My favorite thing is *going* to the beach. (동명사) 내가 가장 좋아하는 것은 해변에 가는 것이다.
> They *are going* to the beach. (현재진행형) 그들은 해변에 가는 중이다.

CHECK UP

● 빈칸에 알맞은 말을 <u>모두</u> 고르시오.

1 Tom and Sera enjoy _____ badminton. ☐ playing ☐ to play

2 What do you want _____ tonight? ☐ doing ☐ to do

3 He finished _____ the report. ☐ writing ☐ to write

4 I like _____ by train. ☐ traveling ☐ to travel

5 He plans _____ to Spain in August. ☐ going ☐ to go

6 The man kept _____ to us. ☐ talking ☐ to talk

7 Eric decided _____ to another city. ☐ moving ☐ to move

8 My father quit _____ a year ago. ☐ smoking ☐ to smoke

9 I started _____ Chinese. ☐ learning ☐ to learn

10 We hope _____ Venice next month. ☐ visiting ☐ to visit

box 안의 예문을 참고하여 우리말과 일치하도록 문장을 완성하시오.

WRITING POINT ①

• **Driving** in the rain is dangerous. 운전하는 것은 / 빗 속에서 / 위험하다

1 춤을 추는 것은 매우 재미있다. _____ is great fun.

2 하루 종일 집에 있는 것은 지루하다. _____ at home all day is boring.

3 새로운 곳들을 방문하는 것은 흥분된다. _____ new places is exciting.

4 매일 운동하는 것은 쉽지 않다. _____ every day is not easy.

5 충분한 물을 마시는 것은 너에게 좋다. _____ enough water is good for you.

WRITING POINT ②

• His hobby is **playing** badminton. 그의 취미는 / 이다 / 배드민턴을 치는 것

1 내 취미는 사진을 찍는 것이다. My hobby is _____ pictures.

2 그의 직업은 버스를 운전하는 것이다. His job is _____ a bus.

3 내 목표는 새로운 언어를 배우는 것이다. My goal is _____ a new language.

4 내 꿈은 외국에서 공부하는 것이다. My dream is _____ abroad.

5 내가 가장 좋아하는 것은 농구하는 것이다. My favorite thing is _____ basketball.

WRITING POINT ③

• She enjoys **listening** to classical music. 그녀는 / 즐긴다 / 듣는 것을 / 클래식 음악을

1 나는 영화 보는 것을 즐긴다. I enjoy _____ movies.

2 그 아기는 계속 울었다. The baby kept _____.

3 그녀는 밤 늦게 먹는 것을 피한다. She avoids _____ late at night.

4 그는 남을 돕는 것을 개의치 않는다. He doesn't mind _____ others.

5 그들은 숙제 하는 것을 끝냈다. They finished _____ their homework.

SENTENCE PRACTICE 2

우리말과 일치하도록 빈칸에 알맞은 말을 넣으시오.

• 동명사: 주어 역할 •

1 문자메시지를 보내는 것은 쉽고 빠르다. (text)

→ _____ is easy and quick.

2 쉽게 포기하는 것은 나쁜 습관이다. (give up)

→ _____ _____ _____ is a bad habit.

3 집을 짓는 것은 많은 시간이 필요하다. (a house)

→ _____ _____ _____ takes a lot of time.

• 동명사: 보어 역할 •

4 그의 성공 비결은 늘 최선을 다하는 것이다. (do his best)

→ His secret to success is always _____ _____ _____.

5 내가 가장 좋아하는 것은 식후에 아이스크림을 먹는 것이다. (ice cream)

→ My favorite thing is _____ _____ _____ after a meal.

6 내 목표는 매일 5킬로미터를 달리는 것이다. (5 kilometers)

→ My goal is _____ _____ _____ every day.

• 동명사: 목적어 역할 •

7 나는 여가 시간에 하이킹 가는 것을 즐긴다. (go hiking)

→ I _____ _____ _____ in my free time.

8 그 수리공은 내 차 수리하는 것을 끝냈다. (fix)

→ The mechanic _____ _____ _____ _____.

9 그는 그의 직업에 대해 계속 불평했다. (complain)

→ He _____ _____ about his job.

10 Peter는 살 빼는 것을 포기했다. (lose weight)

→ Peter _____ _____ _____ _____.

TRY WRITING

동명사와 ( ) 안의 말을 이용하여 우리말을 영어로 옮기시오.

1 그녀의 직업은 아픈 사람들을 돕는 것이다. (sick)

2 영어 소설을 읽는 것은 쉽지 않다. (English novels)

3 나는 가끔씩 혼자 있는 것을 즐긴다. (sometimes / be alone)

4 내 꿈은 언젠가 그 영화배우를 만나는 것이다. (the movie star / one day)

5 그들은 수업 중에 계속 떠들었다. (talk / during the class)

6 슬프게도, 지나(Jina)는 음악 학교에 가는 것을 포기했다. (sadly / music school)

7 매일 일기를 쓰는 것은 좋은 습관이다. (keep a diary / habit)

8 내 목표는 수학에서 좋은 점수를 얻는 것이다. (a good score / in math)

9 충분한 수면을 취하는 것은 당신의 건강에 중요하다. (get enough sleep / for)

10 나는 <해리포터 시리즈> 읽는 것을 끝냈다. (the *Harry Potter* series)

11 너는 너무 많은 정크푸드를 먹는 것을 피해야 한다. (should / avoid / too much)

12 인터넷 검색은 때로는 시간 낭비이다. (surf the Internet / a waste of time)

1 우리말과 같은 뜻이 되도록 주어진 단어를 바르게 배열하시오.

(1) 이 강에서 수영하는 것은 위험하다.
(dangerous / is / river / it / in / to / this / swim)

→ _____

(2) 물 없이 사는 것은 불가능하다.
(water / is / live / to / impossible / without / it)

→ _____

2 주어진 단어를 이용하여 다음 대화의 밑줄 친 우리말을 영작하시오.

A What is your dream?
B 내 꿈은 유명한 가수가 되는 거야.
(be, famous)

→ My dream is _____ _____
_____ _____ _____.

3 다음은 Tom의 이번 주 계획이다. 표를 보고 주어진 문장을 완성하시오.

Mon.	수학 공부하기
Tue.	go to the movies
Wed.	테니스 치기
Thu.	visit his grandmother
Fri.	친구들 만나기

(1) Tom plans _____ _____
_____ on Monday.

(2) Tom plans _____ _____
_____ on Wednesday.

(3) Tom plans _____ _____
_____ _____ on Friday.

4 주어진 단어를 이용하여 우리말을 영작하시오.

그는 함께 놀 친구들이 없다. (no, play with)

→ He has _____ _____
_____ _____ _____.

5 그림을 보고 to부정사를 사용하여 목적을 나타내는 문장을 완성하시오.

(1) He went to the restaurant _____.
(2) She went to the park _____.

6 우리말과 같은 뜻이 되도록 빈칸에 알맞은 말을 쓰시오.

(1) 너무 많이 자는 것은 건강에 좋지 않다.
→ _____ too much is not healthy.

(2) 농구하는 것은 재미있다.
→ _____ _____ is fun.

7 ( ) 안의 단어를 알맞게 고쳐 문장을 완성하시오.

(1) Jane wants _____ the book. (buy)

(2) Ryan enjoys _____ in winter. (ski)

(3) I need _____ him an email. (send)

(4) He finished _____ his homework. (do)

UNIT
08

형용사와 부사

LESSON 20 수량 형용사, 빈도부사

1 수량 형용사에는 **many, much, a lot of/lots of** 등이 있다. 이 형용사들은 명사 앞에서 '많은'이란 의미로 쓰인다.

many + 셀 수 있는 명사 (복수형)	many students, many books, many problems 등
much + 셀 수 없는 명사	much water, much sugar, much money, much time 등
a lot of/lots of + 셀 수 있는 명사 (복수형) 셀 수 없는 명사	a lot of friends, a lot of pens 등 a lot of food, a lot of work 등

PLUS many와 much는 주로 부정문과 의문문에, a lot of/lots of는 주로 긍정문에 쓰인다.

e.g. He doesn't have *much* free time. 그에게는 자유 시간이 많지 않다.
Are there *many* students in your class? 너희 반에는 학생이 많이 있니?
She reads *a lot of* English books. 그녀는 영어 책을 많이 읽는다.

2 빈도부사는 어떤 일을 얼마나 자주 하는지를 나타내는 부사이다. 빈도부사가 문장 내에 쓰인 경우, 동사의 종류에 따라 빈도부사의 위치를 주의해야 한다.

빈도부사의 종류	always(항상), usually(보통), often(자주, 종종), sometimes(때때로), hardly(거의 ~않는), never(결코 ~않는)
빈도부사의 위치	be동사와 조동사 뒤, 일반동사 앞

I **often** *go* to the mall with my friends. 나는 종종 내 친구들과 쇼핑몰에 간다.
He *is* **never** late for work. 그는 결코 직장에 늦지 않는다.
You *must* **always** be home by 10 o'clock. 너는 항상 10시까지 집에 와야 한다.

CHECK UP

● 빈칸에 알맞은 수량 형용사를 고르시오.

1 There aren't _____ cars on the road. ☐ many ☐ much

2 She put too _____ salt in her soup. ☐ many ☐ much

3 _____ people can't find jobs these days. ☐ Many ☐ Much

4 We don't have _____ money now. ☐ many ☐ much

● ( ) 안의 빈도부사가 들어갈 위치에 ∨표 하시오.

5 He is angry with me. (often)

6 I get up late on the weekend. (usually)

7 You should watch out for cars. (always)

8 I will make the same mistake. (never)

box 안의 예문을 참고하여 우리말과 일치하도록 문장을 완성하시오.

WRITING POINT ①

- Are there **many books** in the library? 있니 / 많은 책이 / 그 도서관에?
- He doesn't drink **much coffee**. 그는 / 마시지 않는다 / 많은 커피를

1	공원에 사람들이 많이 있니?	Are there _____ in the park?
2	너는 오늘 숙제가 많니?	Do you have _____ today?
3	나는 입을 옷이 많지 않다.	I don't have _____ to wear.
4	우리에게는 시간이 많지 않다.	We don't have _____.

WRITING POINT ②

- My brother has **a lot of toys**. 내 남동생은 / 가지고 있다 / 많은 장난감들을
- There is **a lot of milk** in the fridge. 있다 / 많은 우유가 / 냉장고에

1	John은 친구들이 많다.	John has _____.
2	Sally는 차를 많이 마신다.	Sally drinks _____.
3	그들은 많은 질문들을 했다.	They asked _____.
4	우리는 많은 음식을 샀다.	We bought _____.

WRITING POINT ③

- I **often skip** breakfast. 나는 / 종종 / 거른다 / 아침을
- She **is always** nice to everyone. 그녀는 / 항상 친절하다 / 모두에게
- You **should never be** late for class. 너는 / 절대로 늦으면 안 된다 / 수업에

1	나는 보통 걸어서 학교에 간다.	I _____ to school.
2	너는 자주 운동을 하니?	Do you _____?
3	그의 방은 항상 깨끗하다.	His room _____ clean.
4	나는 절대로 그를 다시 보지 않을 거야.	I _____ him again.
5	너는 언제나 내 컴퓨터를 사용할 수 있다.	You _____ my computer.

우리말과 일치하도록 빈칸에 알맞은 말을 넣으시오.

• many / much •

I 그녀는 고기를 많이 먹지 않는다. (meat)

→ She _____ _____ _____ _____ .

2 나는 너에게 할 말이 아주 많다. (things)

→ I have so _____ _____ _____ _____ you.

3 작년 여름에는 비가 많이 오지 않았다. (have / rain)

→ We _____ _____ _____ _____ last summer.

4 오늘 밤은 하늘에서 별을 많이 볼 수 없다. (stars)

→ I _____ _____ _____ _____ in the sky tonight.

• a lot of •

5 산 위에 눈이 많이 있다. (snow)

→ There is _____ _____ _____ _____ on the mountains.

6 우리는 해결해야 할 문제들이 많이 있다. (problems)

→ We have _____ _____ _____ _____ to solve.

7 Jessica는 그녀의 생일에 많은 카드를 받았다. (cards)

→ Jessica got _____ _____ _____ _____ on her birthday.

• 빈도부사 •

8 런던은 종종 날씨가 흐리다. (cloudy)

→ It _____ _____ _____ in London.

9 내 차는 때때로 고장 난다. (break down)

→ My car _____ _____ _____ .

10 너는 항상 정직해야 한다. (should)

→ You _____ _____ _____ honest.

( ) 안의 말을 이용하여 우리말을 영어로 옮기시오.

1 나는 보통 밤 10시 전에 잠자리에 든다. (go to bed / 10 p.m.)

2 너는 단것을 너무 많이 먹으면 안 된다. (should / sweets)

3 우리에게는 그 일을 끝낼 시간이 많지 않다. (we / to finish)

4 너무 많은 사랑은 때로는 아이들에게 좋지 않다. (bad for)

5 세계 역사에 대한 많은 책들이 있다. (there / on world history)

6 나는 그 축제에서 많은 외국인들을 만났다. (foreigners / at the festival)

7 그 호텔에는 손님들이 많지 않았다. (there / guests / at the hotel)

8 나의 아버지는 직장에서 늘 바쁘시다. (at work)

9 그는 결코 고맙다는 말을 하지 않는다. (say "thank you")

10 그녀는 옷에 너무 많은 돈을 쓴다. (spend / on clothes)

11 너는 언제든지 나에게 도움을 청해도 돼. (can / ask me for help)

12 너는 네 건강을 위해 야채를 많이 먹어야 한다. (should / vegetables)

LESSON 21 비교급, 최상급

1 비교급과 **최상급**은 형용사나 부사 뒤에 **-er/-est**를 붙이거나 앞에 **more/most**를 붙여 만든다. 비교급 뒤에는 **than**을 쓰고, 최상급 앞에는 정관사 **the**를 붙인다.

비교급	형용사/부사의 비교급 + than	I am taller than you. 나는 너보다 키가 더 크다. Health is more important than money. 건강은 돈보다 더 중요하다.
최상급	the + 형용사/부사의 최상급	Seoul is the biggest city in Korea. 서울은 한국에서 가장 큰 도시이다. The ring is the most expensive of all. 그 반지는 모든 것들 중 가장 비싸다.

2 비교급과 최상급 만드는 방법

규칙 변화	대부분의 형용사/부사	+ er/est	old-older-oldest, fast-faster-fastest
	-e로 끝나는 경우	+ r/st	large-larger-largest
	「자음 + y」로 끝나는 경우	y → i + er/est	easy-easier-easiest
	「단모음 + 단자음」으로 끝나는 경우	마지막 자음 추가 + er/est	big-bigger-biggest, hot-hotter-hottest, thin-thinner-thinnest
	2음절 이상의 형용사/부사, -ful, -ous, -ing, -ive로 끝나는 경우	more/most + 형용사/부사의 원급	popular-**more** popular-**most** popular, boring-**more** boring-**most** boring
불규칙 변화	bad-**worse**-**worst**, good/well-**better**-**best**, many-**more**-**most**, little-**less**-**least**		

CHECK UP

● 다음 형용사/부사의 비교급과 최상급을 순서대로 쓰시오.

1 long _____ _____

2 good _____ _____

3 cute _____ _____

4 difficult _____ _____

5 early _____ _____

6 many _____ _____

7 young _____ _____

8 hot _____ _____

9 interesting _____ _____

10 popular _____ _____

box 안의 예문을 참고하여 우리말과 일치하도록 문장을 완성하시오.

WRITING POINT ①

- Trains are **slower** than airplanes. 기차는 / 더 느리다 / 비행기보다
- Your dress is **more beautiful** than mine. 너의 드레스는 / 더 아름답다 / 내 것보다

1 Tom은 Mike보다 키가 더 작다. Tom is _____ than Mike.

2 인도는 영국보다 더 덥다. India is _____ than England.

3 내 가방은 네 것보다 더 무겁다. My bag is _____ than yours.

4 나에게, 영어는 수학보다 더 쉽다. For me, English is _____ than math.

5 나는 내 여동생보다 일찍 일어난다. I get up _____ than my sister.

6 그 영화는 그 책보다 더 지루하다. The movie is _____ than the book.

7 이 케이크는 저것보다 더 맛있다. This cake is _____ than that one.

8 축구는 골프보다 더 흥미진진하다. Soccer is _____ than golf.

WRITING POINT ②

- My brother is the **tallest** person in my family. 나의 형은 / 이다 / 가장 키가 큰 사람 / 나의 가족 중
- He is the **most popular** actor in Korea. 그는 / 이다 / 가장 인기 있는 배우 / 한국에서

1 1월은 1년 중 가장 추운 달이다. January is the _____ month of the year.

2 Nick은 그 팀에서 가장 빠른 선수이다. Nick is the _____ player on the team.

3 David는 그 반에서 최고의 학생이다. David is the _____ student in the class.

4 Sally는 셋 중 가장 어리다. Sally is the _____ of the three.

5 나일강은 세계에서 가장 긴 강이다. The Nile is the _____ river in the world.

6 이 차는 그 매장에서 가장 비싸다. This car is the _____ in the shop.

7 이 문제는 모든 문제들 중 가장 어렵다. This question is the _____ of all.

8 상어는 바다에서 가장 위험한 동물이다. Sharks are the _____ animals in the sea.

우리말과 일치하도록 빈칸에 알맞은 말을 넣으시오.

• 비교급 + than •

1 내 컴퓨터는 네 것보다 더 새것이다. (new)

→ My computer _____ _____ _____ yours.

2 망고는 오렌지보다 더 달다. (sweet)

→ Mangos _____ _____ _____ oranges.

3 백설공주는 그 마녀보다 더 아름답다. (beautiful)

→ Snow White _____ _____ _____ _____ the witch.

4 나의 아빠는 엄마보다 요리를 더 잘하신다. (cook)

→ My dad _____ _____ _____ my mom.

5 그 반에는 여자아이가 남자아이보다 더 많다. (girls / boys)

→ There are _____ _____ _____ _____ in the class.

• the + 최상급 •

6 그는 세계에서 가장 부유한 사람이다. (rich / person)

→ He is _____ _____ _____ in the world.

7 오늘은 내 인생에서 가장 행복한 날이다. (happy)

→ Today is _____ _____ _____ in my life.

8 나에게, 과학은 가장 어려운 과목이다. (subject)

→ For me, science is _____ _____ _____ _____ .

9 이곳은 마을에서 가장 저렴한 식당이다. (cheap)

→ This is _____ _____ _____ in the town.

10 그것은 공항까지 가는 가장 빠른 방법이다. (quick)

→ It is _____ _____ _____ to get to the airport.

( ) 안의 말을 이용하여 우리말을 영어로 옮기시오.

1 나는 내 여동생보다 머리가 더 길다. (have / hair)

2 나의 할머니는 나의 가족 중 가장 나이가 많은 사람이다. (person / in my family)

3 오늘은 어제보다 더 따뜻하다. (warm)

4 Kate는 Diana보다 더 예쁘다. (pretty)

5 그는 세계에서 가장 빨리 달리는 사람이다. (runner)

6 거북이는 다른 동물들보다 더 오래 산다. (turtles / other animals)

7 첫 번째 문제는 두 번째 문제보다 더 어렵다. (first / second)

8 이곳은 그 도시에서 가장 비싼 호텔이다. (this / in the city)

9 세계에서 가장 높은 산은 어디입니까? (what / high)

10 스키는 낚시보다 더 위험하다. (skiing / fishing)

11 아이스하키는 캐나다에서 가장 인기 있는 스포츠이다. (ice hockey / popular)

12 네 인생에서 가장 중요한 것은 무엇이니? (thing / in your life)

LESSON 22 원급 비교

1 원급 비교는 「as+형용사/부사의 원급+as」 형태로 쓰고 '~만큼 …한'으로 해석한다.

Alan is **as tall as** Linda. Alan은 Linda만큼 키가 크다.
I can sing **as well as** Mary. 나는 Mary만큼 노래를 잘 부를 수 있다.

2 원급 비교의 부정형은 「not as+형용사/부사의 원급+as」이고 '~만큼 …하지 않은'으로 해석한다.

Today is **not as cold as** yesterday. 오늘은 어제만큼 춥지 않다.
Dogs **don't** live **as long as** humans. 개는 사람만큼 오래 살지 않는다.

CHECK UP

● 빈칸에 알맞은 말을 고르시오.

1 The bus is not as _____ as the subway. ☐ fast ☐ faster

2 My cat is _____ than my dog. ☐ fat ☐ fatter

3 This flower is as _____ as that one. ☐ beautiful ☐ more beautiful

4 My sister is _____ than my mother. ☐ tall ☐ taller

5 Steve is as _____ as his father. ☐ strong ☐ stronger

6 The diamond is the _____ mineral. ☐ hard ☐ hardest

7 English is not as _____ as Chinese. ☐ difficult ☐ more difficult

8 Bicycles are _____ than motorcycles. ☐ safe ☐ safer

9 Rome is the _____ city in Italy. ☐ large ☐ largest

10 The weather today is _____ than yesterday. ☐ bad ☐ worse

box 안의 예문을 참고하여 우리말과 일치하도록 문장을 완성하시오.

WRITING POINT ❶

• The red car is **as fast as** the blue car. 빨간 자동차는 / 빠르다 / 파란 자동차만큼

1 이 침대는 돌처럼 딱딱하다.   This bed is _____ a rock.

2 그녀의 피부는 눈처럼 하얗다.   Her skin is _____ snow.

3 그 물은 얼음처럼 차갑다.   The water is _____ ice.

4 시간은 돈만큼 중요하다.   Time is _____ money.

5 그 담요는 깃털만큼 가볍다.   The blanket is _____ a feather.

6 이 피자는 그 파스타만큼 맛있다.   This pizza is _____ the pasta.

7 이 문제는 ABC만큼이나 쉽다.   This problem is _____ ABC.

8 그는 너만큼 많이 먹는다.   He eats _____ you.

9 Jane은 Jim만큼 테니스를 잘 친다.   Jane plays tennis _____ Jim.

WRITING POINT ❷

• Jack is **not as friendly as** his brother. Jack은 / 친절하지 않다 / 그의 남동생만큼

1 내 머리는 너의 것만큼 길지 않다.   My hair is _____ yours.

2 은은 금만큼 무겁지 않다.   Silver is _____ gold.

3 달은 태양만큼 밝지 않다.   The moon is _____ the sun.

4 그리스는 프랑스만큼 크지 않다.   Greece is _____ France.

5 배구는 축구만큼 인기 있지 않다.   Volleyball is _____ soccer.

6 올 여름은 작년 여름만큼 덥지 않다.   This summer is _____ last summer.

7 그의 아이디어는 네 것만큼 좋지 않다. His idea is _____ yours.

8 이 그림은 저것만큼 오래되지 않았다. This painting is _____ that one.

9 John은 Mark만큼 열심히 일하지 않는다. John doesn't work _____ Mark.

우리말과 일치하도록 빈칸에 알맞은 말을 넣으시오.

• as + 형용사/부사 원급 + as •

I   Bill은 그의 아버지만큼 키가 크다. (tall)

→ Bill is _____ _____ _____ _____ _____.

2   그 팔찌는 그 목걸이만큼 비싸다. (expensive)

→ The bracelet _____ _____ _____ _____ the necklace.

3   이 새로 산 소파는 예전 것만큼 편하다. (comfortable)

→ This new sofa _____ _____ _____ _____ the old one.

4   나는 너만큼 자전거를 잘 탈 수 있다. (well)

→ I can ride a bike _____ _____ _____ _____.

5   나는 내가 할 수 있는 만큼 자주 운동하려고 노력한다. (often)

→ I try to exercise _____ _____ _____ _____ _____.

• not as + 형용사/부사 원급 + as •

6   나는 너만큼 피곤하지 않다. (tired)

→ I _____ _____ _____ _____ _____ you.

7   호수는 바다만큼 크지 않다. (big)

→ A lake _____ _____ _____ _____ _____ an ocean.

8   돈은 건강만큼 중요하지 않다. (important)

→ Money _____ _____ _____ _____ _____ good health.

9   타조는 치타만큼 빠르게 달릴 수 없다. (fast)

→ Ostriches cannot _____ _____ _____ _____ cheetahs.

10   그 버스는 평소만큼 붐비지 않았다. (crowded)

→ The bus _____ _____ _____ _____ _____ usual.

( ) 안의 말을 이용하여 우리말을 영어로 옮기시오.

1   나의 어머니는 나의 아버지만큼 나이가 많다. (old)

2   그 나무는 그 집만큼 높지 않다. (tall)

3   이 블라우스는 실크만큼 부드럽다. (smooth / silk)

4   나는 너만큼 높이 뛸 수 있다. (can / jump / high)

5   Paul은 Steve만큼 춤을 잘 추지 못한다. (can / dance)

6   모차르트(Mozart)는 베토벤(Beethoven)만큼 훌륭했다. (great)

7   Tom은 Jerry만큼 영리하지 않다. (clever)

8   그는 그가 할 수 있는 만큼 빨리 달리고 있다. (fast / he can)

9   이 사과는 저것보다 달지 않다. (that one)

10   그 새 신발은 오래된 것만큼 편하지 않다. (the new shoes / the old ones)

11   나는 TV를 너만큼 많이 보지 않는다. (watch TV)

12   그 새로 오신 선생님은 김 선생님만큼이나 좋다. (nice / Mr. Kim)

1 각 문장의 빈칸에 적절한 단어를 〈보기〉에서 한 번씩 만 사용하여 문장을 완성하시오.

보기   a lot of / many / much

(1) 그녀는 채소를 많이 먹지 않는다.

→ She doesn't eat _____ vegetables.

(2) 네 수프에 소금을 너무 많이 넣지 마.

→ Don't put too _____ salt in your soup.

(3) 민호는 친구들이 많다.

→ Minho has _____ friends.

2 주어진 단어를 이용하여 문장을 완성하시오.

(1) Amy는 Emily보다 더 많은 책을 가지고 있다. (many)

→ Amy has _____ _____ than Emily.

(2) 나에게, 영어가 중국어보다 쉽다. (easy)

→ For me, English is _____ _____ Chinese.

3 그림을 보고 빈칸에 알맞은 말을 쓰시오. (단, 형용사로 expensive를 사용할 것)

(1) The dress is _____ _____ the bag.

(2) The pants are _____ _____ _____ of the three.

4 주어진 단어를 이용하여 우리말을 영작하시오.

(1) 내 여동생은 나의 가족 중 가장 키가 작다. (sister, short)

→ _____

(2) 세계에서 가장 큰 동물은 무엇입니까? (what, large)

→ _____

5 다음은 세 사람의 키이다. 표를 보고 아래 질문에 대한 답을 7단어의 완전한 문장으로 쓰시오.

Jisu	Sora	Misun
160cm	163cm	158cm

Q Who is the tallest of the three?

A _____

6 주어진 정보를 활용하여 같은 의미가 되도록 빈칸에 알맞은 말을 쓰시오.

· Inseong weighs 50kg.
· Dongho weighs 50kg, too.

→ Inseong is _____ _____ _____ Dongho.

7 그림을 보고 주어진 단어를 이용하여 문장을 완성하시오.

→ The horse can _____. (run, fast, as)

UNIT
09

전치사, 접속사

LESSON 23 전치사

1 전치사는 명사나 명사구 앞에 놓여 시간, 장소, 방향, 위치 등을 나타낼 수 있다. 대표적인 **시간 전치사**에는 **in, on, at**이 있다.

in (월, 계절, 연도 등)	on (요일, 날짜, 특정일)	at (시각, 특정 시점)
in April 4월에 in summer 여름에 in 2020 2020년에 in the morning 아침에	on Sunday(s) 일요일에(마다) on November 5th 11월 5일에 on Sunday morning 일요일 아침에 on Christmas (day) 크리스마스 날에	at 7 o'clock 7시에 at noon 정오에 at night 밤에 at Christmas 크리스마스 연휴에

PLUS on Christmas (day) vs. at Christmas
일반적으로 크리스마스 당일은 on Christmas (day)를 쓰고, 연휴 등을 포함한 크리스마스 기간은 at Christmas를 쓴다.

e.g. The baby was born *on Christmas day*. 그 아기는 크리스마스 날에 태어났다.
Many people go shopping *at Christmas*. 많은 사람들이 크리스마스 연휴에 쇼핑을 하러 간다.

2 **in, on, at**은 장소 전치사로도 쓰인다. 이 외에 장소나 위치를 나타내는 전치사에는 **under, in front of, behind, next to, between** 등이 있다.

in	실내 / 넓은 장소	in front of	~ 앞에
at	특정 지점	behind	~ 뒤에
on	~ (표면) 위에	next to	~ 옆에
under	~ 아래에	between	~ 사이에

CHECK UP

● 빈칸에 알맞은 시간 전치사를 고르시오.

1 I am going to visit Paris _____ July. ☐ in ☐ at

2 They came back home _____ 9:30. ☐ on ☐ at

3 She entered middle school _____ 2015. ☐ in ☐ at

4 Goodbye! See you _____ Monday. ☐ in ☐ on

● 빈칸에 알맞은 장소 전치사를 고르시오.

5 Jack and Jill met _____ Seattle. ☐ in ☐ on

6 There is a mirror _____ the wall. ☐ on ☐ at

7 The river flows _____ the bridge. ☐ on ☐ under

8 The hospital is _____ the bank and the library. ☐ at ☐ between

box 안의 예문을 참고하여 우리말과 일치하도록 문장을 완성하시오.

WRITING POINT ①

• He was born **on** July 10, 1982. 그는 / 태어났다 / 1982년 7월 10일에

1 학교는 3시에 끝난다. School is over _____ 3 o'clock.

2 나는 아침에 일찍 일어난다. I get up early _____ the morning.

3 그는 토요일마다 테니스를 친다. He plays tennis _____ Saturdays.

4 우리는 정오에 점심을 먹는다. We have lunch _____ noon.

5 그녀의 생일은 1월에 있다. Her birthday is _____ January.

6 그 공연은 8월 24일에 있다. The concert is _____ August 24th.

7 그는 2010년에 서울로 이사 갔다. They moved to Seoul _____ 2010.

8 나는 겨울에 종종 스키를 타러 간다. I often go skiing _____ winter.

9 박쥐들은 밤에 사냥한다. Bats hunt _____ night.

WRITING POINT ②

• They are playing **in** the park. 그들은 / 놀고 있다 / 공원에서

1 나의 삼촌은 캐나다에 산다. My uncle lives _____ Canada.

2 의자에 앉으세요. Please sit _____ the chair.

3 그녀는 부엌에서 요리 중이다. She is cooking _____ the kitchen.

4 그녀는 버스 정류장에 서 있다. She is standing _____ the bus stop.

5 그들은 나무 아래서 쉬고 있다. They are resting _____ the tree.

6 한 남자가 내 옆에 앉았다. A man sat _____ me.

7 주차장은 그 건물 뒤에 있다. The parking lot is _____ the building.

8 그 버스는 호텔 앞에 정차한다. The bus stops _____ the hotel.

9 그 탁자는 침대 사이에 있다. The table is _____ the beds.

우리말과 일치하도록 빈칸에 알맞은 말을 넣으시오.

• 시간의 전치사 •

1 그 연극은 7시 30분에 시작한다. (7:30)

→ The play begins _____ _____ .

2 내 언니의 결혼식은 금요일에 있다. (Friday)

→ My sister's wedding is _____ _____ .

3 우리는 봄에 많은 다른 꽃들을 볼 수 있다. (spring)

→ We can see many different flowers _____ _____ .

4 나는 항상 엄마 생신에 엄마에게 카드를 쓴다. (her birthday)

→ I always write a card to my mom _____ _____ _____ .

5 밤에 혼자 걷는 것은 위험하다. (night)

→ It is dangerous to walk alone _____ _____ .

• 장소/위치의 전치사 •

6 그들은 유럽에서 많은 사진을 찍었다. (Europe)

→ They took a lot of photos _____ _____ .

7 문에 누군가가 있다. (the door)

→ There is someone _____ _____ _____ .

8 내 옆에 있는 남자는 계속 시끄럽게 이야기했다. (me)

→ The man _____ _____ _____ kept talking loudly.

9 나는 거실 소파 위에서 너의 노트북을 봤어.

→ I saw your laptop _____ the sofa _____ the living room.

10 극장 앞에서 5시 반에 만나자. (the theater)

→ Let's meet _____ _____ _____ _____ at 5:30.

( ) 안의 말을 이용하여 우리말을 영어로 옮기시오.

1 7월에는 종종 비가 온다. (it / rain)

2 나의 부모님은 2000년에 결혼하셨다. (get married)

3 천장에 모기 두 마리가 있다. (there / mosquitoes / the ceiling)

4 그들은 식탁에서 저녁 식사를 하고 있다. (have dinner / the table)

5 그녀는 보통 금요일마다 장을 보러 간다. (go grocery shopping / Fridays)

6 그 상점은 일요일 아침에는 10시에 문을 연다. (the shop / 10 o'clock / Sunday morning)

7 토끼 한 마리가 덤불 뒤에 숨어 있다. (a rabbit / hide / the bush)

8 Tim은 어제 자정에 집에 돌아왔다. (come back / midnight)

9 그 배는 다리 밑을 지나가고 있다. (the ship / pass / the bridge)

10 Susan은 정원에서 꽃에 물을 주고 있다. (water / the flowers)

11 학교 첫날에, 나는 새 친구들을 많이 만났다. (the first day of school / a lot of)

12 달은 지구와 태양 사이에 있다. (the moon / the earth / the sun)

접속사

1 접속사는 단어와 단어, 구와 구, 절과 절을 연결하는 역할을 한다. 접속사 **when, before, after, because**는 **부사절**을 이끌어 **때**와 **이유**를 나타낸다.

when	~일 때	When I listen to music, I feel good. 음악을 들을 때, 나는 기분이 좋다.
before	~ 전에	I always brush my teeth before I go to bed. 나는 잠자리에 들기 전에 항상 이를 닦는다.
after	~ 후에	After we finished our homework, we had pizza. 숙제를 끝낸 후에, 우리는 피자를 먹었다.
because	~ 때문에	Everyone likes Jack because he is always nice. Jack은 항상 친절하기 때문에 모두가 그를 좋아한다.

NOTE 부사절이 문장 앞에 오는 경우에는 콤마(,)를 사용한다.

2 **think, believe, know, hope, hear, say** 등의 동사 뒤에 **접속사 that**이 이끄는 **명사절**이 나오면 '~라고', '~라는 것을'의 의미로 쓰인다. 이때 that절은 동사의 **목적어** 역할을 하며, 접속사 that은 **생략**할 수 있다.

I think **(that)** he is a good dancer. 나는 그가 춤을 잘 춘다고 생각해.
We know **(that)** the earth is round. 우리는 지구가 둥글다는 것을 안다.

CHECK UP

● 빈칸에 알맞은 말을 고르시오.

1 I take the bus to school _____ it rains.
☐ that ☐ when

2 A rainbow appears _____ it rains.
☐ before ☐ after

3 He went to bed early _____ he was tired.
☐ because ☐ that

4 I think _____ the shoes are too expensive.
☐ because ☐ that

5 _____ I was young, I lived with my grandfather.
☐ when ☐ after

6 Turn off the lights _____ you leave the room.
☐ that ☐ before

7 _____ he took a shower, he went out.
☐ That ☐ After

8 People believe _____ this story is true.
☐ that ☐ when

9 The lesson ends _____ the bell rings.
☐ that ☐ when

10 I didn't know _____ he was sick yesterday.
☐ that ☐ after

box 안의 예문을 참고하여 우리말과 일치하도록 문장을 완성하시오.

- **When** I was young, I wanted to be a doctor. 내가 어렸을 때 / 나는 원했다 / 의사가 되기를
- I wanted to be a doctor **when** I was young. 나는 원했다 / 의사가 되기를 / 내가 어렸을 때

1 내가 런던에 도착할 때, 너에게 문자 할게. _____ I arrive in London, I'll text you.

2 나는 음악을 들을 때 기분이 좋다. I feel good _____ I listen to music.

3 잠자리에 들기 전에, 나는 책을 읽는다. _____ I go to bed, I read a book.

4 Jack은 저녁을 먹기 전에 운동을 한다. Jack exercises _____ he eats dinner.

5 머리를 감은 후에, 나는 항상 말린다. _____ I wash my hair, I always dry it.

6 그는 대학을 마친 후 직장을 구했다. He got a job _____ he finished college.

7 나는 점심을 먹지 않아서 배가 고프다. I am hungry _____ I didn't eat lunch.

8 아팠기 때문에, 그는 출근하지 않았다. _____ he was sick, he didn't go to work.

- I **think (that)** he is very talented. 나는 / 생각한다 / 그가 매우 재능이 있다고

1 나는 Julie가 예쁘다고 생각해. I _____ Julie is pretty.

2 나는 우리가 경기에서 이길 거라 믿어. I _____ we will win the game.

3 나는 크리스마스 날에 눈이 오길 바란다. I _____ it snows on Christmas day.

4 우리는 John이 정직하다는 것을 안다. We _____ John is honest.

5 나는 네가 차 사고를 당했다고 들었어. I _____ you had a car accident.

6 그는 그 영화가 환상적이었다고 말했다. He _____ the movie was fantastic.

7 나는 그가 학생이라고 생각했다. I _____ he was a student.

8 나는 네가 한국 음식을 좋아하는지 몰랐어. I _____ you liked Korean food.

9 나는 그가 복권에 당첨되었다는 것을 믿을 수 없다. I _____ he won the lottery.

우리말과 일치하도록 빈칸에 알맞은 말을 넣으시오.

• 부사절 접속사 •

1 우리는 비가 많이 와서 하루 종일 집에 있었다. (it / a lot)

→ We stayed home all day _____ _____ _____ _____ _____.

2 나가기 전에 창문 좀 닫아줄래? (go out)

→ Can you close the window _____ _____ _____ _____?

3 잠이 든 후에, 그는 이상한 꿈을 꿨다. (fall asleep)

→ _____ _____ _____ _____, he had a strange dream.

4 내가 집에 가면 내 개가 나를 맞이해준다. (get home)

→ My dog greets me _____ _____ _____ _____.

5 그 소식을 들었을 때, 그녀는 기뻐서 뛰었다. (hear)

→ _____ _____ _____ _____ _____, she jumped with joy.

• 명사절 접속사 that •

6 나는 그가 유머 감각이 뛰어나다고 생각해.

→ _____ _____ _____ he has a good sense of humor.

7 나는 네가 빨리 낫기를 바라.

→ _____ _____ _____ you will get better soon.

8 우리는 흡연이 우리 건강에 나쁘다는 것을 안다.

→ _____ _____ _____ smoking is bad for our health.

9 사람들은 네 잎 클로버가 그들에게 행운을 가져다 준다고 믿는다.

→ _____ _____ _____ a four-leaf clover brings them good luck.

10 너는 그가 그 팀에서 최고의 선수라고 생각하니?

→ _____ _____ _____ he is the best player on the team?

( ) 안의 말을 이용하여 우리말을 영어로 옮기시오.

1　Jack은 버스를 놓쳐서 학교에 늦었다. (late for / miss / the bus)

2　나는 우리가 숙제가 너무 많다고 생각해. (think / too much)

3　너는 피곤할 때 운전하면 안 된다. (should / tired)

4　그들은 날씨가 너무 추워서 캠핑하러 가지 않았다. (go camping / it / too)

5　나는 감기에 걸렸을 때 뜨거운 차를 마신다. (hot tea / have a cold)

6　나는 네가 좋은 시간 갖기를 바라. (have a good time)

7　나는 그녀가 훌륭한 피아니스트가 될 거라 믿어. (will / be / great)

8　Jane과 Bob은 영화가 시작하기 전에 팝콘을 샀다. (popcorn / start)

9　너는 화성에 생명체가 있다고 생각하니? (there / life / on Mars)

10　나는 잠자리에 들기 전에 항상 샤워를 한다. (take a shower)

11　나는 우리가 그것을 해냈다는 것을 믿을 수 없다. (make it)

12　나는 네가 1등 상을 받은 지 몰랐어. (win / the first prize)

1 다음 빈칸에 알맞은 전치사를 쓰시오.

(1) It snows a lot _____ December.

(2) We usually have dinner _____ 6:30.

2 어법에 맞도록 빈칸에 알맞은 표현을 〈보기〉에서 골라 쓰시오.

보기   summer / July 10 / 2 o'clock

→ The festival begins on _____.

3 밑줄 친 ①~⑤에서 어법상 틀린 곳을 3개 찾아 바르게 고쳐 쓰시오.

My grandmother was born ① at Busan ② in 1950. She usually gets up ③ on 6 a.m. and goes to bed early. She likes growing plants. ④ In spring, she plants a lot of flowers in her garden. She will be 70 next month. I will write her a letter ⑤ in her birthday.

_____ → _____

_____ → _____

_____ → _____

4 주어진 단어를 이용하여 우리말을 영작하시오.

(1) 두 사람이 벤치에 앉아 있다.

(people, sit, the bench)

→ _____

(2) 그 고양이는 가방 뒤에서 자고 있다.

(the cat, sleep, the bag)

→ _____

5 그림을 보고, 〈보기〉에서 적절한 단어를 선택하여 각 인물의 위치를 설명하는 문장을 완성하시오. (단, 〈보기〉의 단어는 한 번씩만 사용할 것)

보기   next to / in front of / between

(1) Lisa is _____.

(2) Mary is _____.

(3) Tom is _____.

6 주어진 단어를 바르게 배열하여 문장을 완성하시오.

(1) (pass / he / test / I / can / the / that / think)

→ _____

(2) (I / we / hope / again / can / that / see)

→ _____

7 다음 두 문장을 (   ) 안에 주어진 단어를 이용하여 한 문장으로 연결하시오.

(1) I learned to ride a bike. I was five. (when)

→ _____

(2) It is raining. We can't play football. (because)

→ _____

UNIT
10

문장의 종류

명령문

1 긍정 명령문은 '~하라'의 의미로 누군가에게 **지시**나 **명령**을 할 때 쓰는 말이다. 명령문은 주어 없이 **동사원형**으로 시작한다.

일반동사 긍정 명령문	<u>Turn</u> off the light. 불을 꺼라. <u>Open</u> your book. 책을 펴라.
be동사 긍정 명령문	<u>Be</u> quiet in the library. 도서관에서는 조용히 해라. <u>Be</u> careful when you cross the road. 길을 건널 때는 조심해라.

2 부정 명령문은 '~하지 마라'의 의미로 긍정 명령문 앞에 **Don't**를 붙여 만든다.

일반동사 부정 명령문	<u>Don't</u> cut in line. 새치기하지 마라. <u>Don't</u> touch it. 그것을 만지지 마라.
be동사 부정 명령문	<u>Don't</u> be late. 늦지 마. <u>Don't</u> be sad. 슬퍼하지 마.

PLUS 명령문에 please를 붙이면 공손한 표현이 된다.
  e.g. *Please* bring me some ice water. 얼음물 좀 갖다 주세요.
      Sit on the chair, *please*. 의자에 앉으세요.

CHECK UP

● 빈칸에 알맞은 말을 고르시오.

l	_____ some lemonade.	☐ Have	☐ Has
2	Always _____ your best.	☐ do	☐ doing
3	_____ careful of your health.	☐ Are	☐ Be
4	_____ me your pen, please.	☐ Lend	☐ Lends
5	Please _____ off the computer.	☐ turn	☐ to turn
6	_____ bring your pet here.	☐ Don't	☐ Doesn't
7	_____ late for the movie.	☐ Be not	☐ Don't be
8	Don't _____ your things on the floor.	☐ leave	☐ leaves
9	_____ be nervous. It's okay.	☐ Isn't	☐ Don't
l0	Please _____ smoke in this building.	☐ not	☐ don't

box 안의 예문을 참고하여 우리말과 일치하도록 문장을 완성하시오.

WRITING POINT ①

- **Come** back home before 8. 집에 돌아와라 / 8시 전에
- **Be** kind to other people. 친절해라 / 다른 사람들에게

1 창문을 닫아라.   _____ the window.

2 우산을 가져가라.   _____ your umbrella.

3 일찍 잠자리에 들어라.   _____ to bed early.

4 자신감을 가져라.   _____ confident.

5 소금 좀 건네주세요.   Please _____ me the salt.

6 들어와서 앉으세요.   Please _____ in and _____ down.

7 방과 후에 숙제를 해라.   _____ your homework after school.

8 6시 전에 네 일을 끝내라.   _____ your work before 6 o'clock.

WRITING POINT ②

- **Don't park** here. 주차하지 마시오 / 여기에
- **Don't be** nervous. 긴장하지 마라

1 너무 크게 말하지 마라.   _____ _____ too loudly.

2 네 남동생과 싸우지 마라.   _____ _____ with your brother.

3 복도에서 뛰지 마라.   _____ _____ in the hallway.

4 음악을 틀지 마라.   _____ _____ the music.

5 부끄러워하지 마라.   _____ _____ shy.

6 그의 말을 듣지 마라.   _____ _____ to him.

7 부모님께 거짓말하지 마라.   _____ _____ lies to your parents.

8 실수하는 걸 두려워하지 마라. _____ _____ afraid of making mistakes.

우리말과 일치하도록 빈칸에 알맞은 말을 넣으시오.

• 긍정 명령문 •

1 그 우유를 냉장고에 넣어라. (put)

→ _____ _____ _____ in the refrigerator.

2 줄을 서세요. (stand)

→ _____ in line, _____.

3 가족들과 좋은 시간 보내. (a good time)

→ _____ _____ _____ _____ with your family.

4 네 여동생에게 항상 잘해 주어라. (nice)

→ Always _____ _____ to your sister.

5 음악 소리 좀 낮춰주세요. (turn down)

→ _____ _____ _____ the music.

• 부정 명령문 •

6 밤에는 시끄럽게 하지 마라. (make noise)

→ _____ _____ _____ at night.

7 햇볕에 너무 오래 있지 마라. (stay)

→ _____ _____ in the sun too long.

8 다시는 늦지 마라. (late)

→ _____ _____ _____ again.

9 네 카메라 가져오는 거 잊지 마. (forget)

→ _____ _____ to bring your camera.

10 그것에 대해 아무에게도 말하지 마. (tell / anybody)

→ _____ _____ _____ about it.

( ) 안의 말을 이용하여 우리말을 영어로 옮기시오.

1 모퉁이에서 우회전해라. (turn / at the corner)

2 침대 위에서 뛰지 마라. (jump)

3 네 휴대전화 잊지 마. (forget)

4 그것들을 안전한 곳에 보관해라. (keep / a safe place)

5 이 약을 하루 세 번 복용해라. (take / medicine / times)

6 TV를 너무 많이 보지 마라. (too much TV)

7 쓰레기를 쓰레기통에 넣어라. (the trash / the trash can)

8 네 선생님에게 무례하게 하지 마라. (rude to)

9 빨간 불일 때는 길을 건너지 마라. (cross / the road / at a red light)

10 발표 중에는 조용히 해주세요. (please / quiet / during the presentation)

11 밤늦게 피아노 치지 마라. (late at night)

12 나가기 전에 자외선 차단제를 발라라. (put sunscreen / before / go out)

1 What 감탄문은 「What(+a/an)+형용사+명사+주어+동사!」의 형태로, '정말 ~하구나!'라는 의미이다. 이때 「주어+동사」는 생략해서 쓰기도 하며, 명사가 **복수형**이거나 **셀 수 없는 명사**일 때는 **a/an**을 쓰지 않는다.

단수명사와 쓰일 때	She is *a very lovely girl*. → What a lovely girl (she is)! 그녀는 정말 사랑스럽구나! He has *a very expensive watch*. → What an expensive watch he has! 그는 정말 비싼 시계를 가지고 있구나!
복수명사와 쓰일 때	They are *very beautiful flowers*. → What beautiful flowers (they are)! 그것들은 정말 아름다운 꽃이구나!

2 How 감탄문은 「How+형용사/부사+주어+동사!」의 형태로, '정말 ~하구나!'라는 의미이다. What 감탄문과는 달리, 명사를 쓰지 않고 how 뒤에 **형용사**나 **부사**가 온다.

형용사와 쓰일 때	He is *very kind*. → How kind (he is)! 그는 정말 친절하구나!
부사와 쓰일 때	She works *very hard*. → How hard she works! 그녀는 정말 열심히 일하는구나!

CHECK UP

● 빈칸에 알맞은 말을 고르시오.

1 _____ beautiful she is! ☐ What ☐ How

2 _____ an amazing show it is! ☐ What ☐ How

3 _____ cute the puppies are! ☐ What ☐ How

4 _____ an expensive car! ☐ What ☐ How

5 _____ sweet you are! ☐ What ☐ How

6 _____ fast the train runs! ☐ What ☐ How

7 _____ big shoes they are! ☐ What ☐ How

8 _____ a great idea you have! ☐ What ☐ How

9 _____ delicious the cake is! ☐ What ☐ How

10 _____ great paintings these are! ☐ What ☐ How

SENTENCE PRACTICE 1

box 안의 예문을 참고하여 우리말과 일치하도록 문장을 완성하시오.

WRITING POINT ①

· **What an interesting book** it is! 정말 흥미로운 책이구나 / 그것은!

1 그것은 정말 큰 물고기구나! ＿＿＿＿＿＿＿＿＿＿＿＿＿＿ it is!

2 그것은 정말 싼 가방이구나! ＿＿＿＿＿＿＿＿＿＿＿＿＿＿ it is!

3 그것은 정말 흥미로운 이야기구나! ＿＿＿＿＿＿＿＿＿＿＿＿＿＿ it is!

4 너는 정말 좋은 언니구나! ＿＿＿＿＿＿＿＿＿＿＿＿＿＿ you are!

5 그들은 정말 좋은 친구들이구나! ＿＿＿＿＿＿＿＿＿＿＿＿＿＿ they are!

6 너는 정말 멋진 모자를 가지고 있구나! ＿＿＿＿＿＿＿＿＿＿＿＿＿＿ you have!

7 그는 정말 큰 집을 가지고 있구나! ＿＿＿＿＿＿＿＿＿＿＿＿＿＿ he has!

8 정말 특별한 하루였어! ＿＿＿＿＿＿＿＿＿＿＿＿＿＿ it was!

9 그는 정말 훌륭한 일을 했구나! ＿＿＿＿＿＿＿＿＿＿＿＿＿＿ he did!

WRITING POINT ②

· **How big** the watermelon is! 정말 크구나 / 그 수박은!

1 그는 정말 잘생겼구나! ＿＿＿＿＿＿＿＿＿ he is!

2 정말 춥구나! ＿＿＿＿＿＿＿＿＿ it is!

3 이 초콜릿은 정말 달콤하구나! ＿＿＿＿＿＿＿＿＿ this chocolate is!

4 너는 정말 용감하구나! ＿＿＿＿＿＿＿＿＿ you are!

5 그것들은 정말 맛있구나! ＿＿＿＿＿＿＿＿＿ they are!

6 그녀는 정말 행복해 보이는구나! ＿＿＿＿＿＿＿＿＿ she looks!

7 그는 정말 빨리 달리는구나! ＿＿＿＿＿＿＿＿＿ he runs!

8 그 시험은 얼마나 어려웠던지! ＿＿＿＿＿＿＿＿＿ the test was!

9 그 석양은 얼마나 아름다웠던지! ＿＿＿＿＿＿＿＿＿ the sunset was!

우리말과 일치하도록 빈칸에 알맞은 말을 넣으시오.

• What 감탄문 •

I   그는 정말 훌륭한 가수구나! (great)

→ What _____ _____ _____ _____ _____!

2   그들은 정말 좋은 이웃들이구나! (neighbors)

→ What _____ _____ _____ _____!

3   그녀는 정말 사랑스러운 미소를 가지고 있구나! (lovely)

→ What _____ _____ _____ _____ _____!

4   너는 정말 멋진 셔츠를 입고 있구나! (nice / wearing)

→ What _____ _____ _____ _____ _____ _____!

5   정말 긴 하루였어! (long / it)

→ What _____ _____ _____ _____ _____!

• How 감탄문 •

6   정말 피곤하구나! (tired / I)

→ How _____ _____ _____!

7   너는 정말 바쁘구나! (busy)

→ How _____ _____ _____!

8   너희 개는 정말 똑똑하구나! (smart)

→ How _____ _____ _____ _____!

9   그는 정말 천천히 말하는구나! (slowly)

→ How _____ _____ _____!

10   그녀는 정말 아름답게 춤추는구나! (beautifully)

→ How _____ _____ _____!

( ) 안의 말을 이용하여 우리말을 영어로 옮기시오.

1 김 선생님은 정말 친절하시구나! (kind / Mr. Kim)

2 정말 더운 날이야! (a hot day)

3 그 식당은 정말 싸구나! (cheap / the restaurant)

4 그 거리들은 정말 깨끗하구나! (clean / the streets)

5 그것은 정말 유용한 정보구나! (a useful tip)

6 너는 정말 예쁜 가방을 가지고 있구나! (a pretty bag)

7 그녀는 정말 아름다워 보이는구나! (beautiful / look)

8 그것은 정말 훌륭한 연설이었어! (a great speech)

9 그 여행은 정말 멋졌어! (wonderful / the trip)

10 그것은 정말 흥미진진한 경기였어! (an exciting game)

11 그는 정말 빨리 달리고 있구나! (fast / running)

12 너는 정말 멋진 사진들을 찍었구나! (nice pictures / take)

부가의문문

▎ **부가의문문**은 '그렇지?' 또는 '그렇지 않니?'란 뜻으로, 말한 내용을 확인하거나 동의를 구하기 위해 평서문 뒤에 덧붙이는 의문문이다. 부가의문문을 만드는 방법은 다음과 같다.

(1) 부가의문문은 앞 문장이 긍정이면 부정으로, 부정이면 긍정으로 만든다.

(2) 부가의문문의 주어는 인칭대명사(I, we, you, he, she, it, they)를 쓴다.

(3) 앞 문장의 동사 종류에 따라 부가의문문의 동사가 달라진다.

   (be동사 → be동사, 조동사 → 조동사, 일반동사 → do/does/did)

be동사의 부가의문문	*It is* a cold day, isn't it? 추운 날이구나, 그렇지 않니? *They are not* hungry, are they? 그들은 배가 고프지 않아, 그렇지?
조동사의 부가의문문	*David can* swim well, can't he? David는 수영을 잘해, 그렇지 않니? *You won't go* there, will you? 너는 거기에 가지 않을 거야, 그렇지?
일반동사의 부가의문문	*Sora lives* in Seoul, doesn't she? 소라는 서울에 살아, 그렇지 않니? *You didn't have* lunch, *did you*? 너는 점심을 먹지 않았어, 그렇지 않니?

NOTE 부가의문문에 대한 대답은 일반 의문문과 마찬가지로 내용이 긍정이면 Yes, 부정이면 No로 답한다.
e.g. A: Taeho is in your class, isn't he? 태호는 너희 반이야, 그렇지 않니?
B: Yes, he is. 응, 맞아. / No, he isn't. 아니, 그렇지 않아.

PLUS 명령문의 부가의문문은 'will you?', Let's로 시작하는 문장의 부가의문문은 'shall we?'를 쓴다.
e.g. Study hard, *will you*? 열심히 공부할 거지?
Let's start now, *shall we*? 이제 출발할까?

CHECK UP

● 빈칸에 알맞은 말을 고르시오.

1 They are your friends, _____? ☐ are they ☐ aren't they

2 Susan has a car, _____? ☐ does she ☐ doesn't she

3 You can speak Chinese, _____? ☐ don't you ☐ can't you

4 Your father is a lawyer, _____? ☐ is he ☐ isn't he

5 Eddie, you used my pen, _____? ☐ didn't he ☐ didn't you

6 They didn't have breakfast, _____? ☐ did they ☐ didn't they

7 She was your neighbor, _____? ☐ isn't she ☐ wasn't she

8 Joe and Lisa weren't at school, _____? ☐ were they ☐ weren't they

9 I should tell the teacher, _____? ☐ should I ☐ shouldn't I

10 Kevin doesn't eat onions, _____? ☐ does he ☐ doesn't he

box 안의 예문을 참고하여 우리말과 일치하도록 문장을 완성하시오.

WRITING POINT ❶

• The garden is beautiful, **isn't it**? 그 정원은 아름다워 / 그렇지 않니?

1	그녀는 노래를 잘해, 그렇지 않니?	She is a good singer, _____?
2	넌 내 가장 친한 친구야, 그렇지 않니?	You are my best friend, _____?
3	우리는 늦지 않았어, 그렇지?	We are not late, _____?
4	그들은 집에 없었어, 그렇지?	They weren't at home, _____?
5	그 영화는 지루했어, 그렇지 않니?	The movie was boring, _____?

WRITING POINT ❷

• You can play the guitar, **can't you**? 너는 기타를 연주할 수 있어 / 그렇지 않니?

1	그녀는 영어를 할 수 있어, 그렇지 않니?	She can speak English, _____?
2	Tim은 운전을 못해, 그렇지?	Tim can't drive a car, _____?
3	너는 도서관에 가지 않을 거야, 그렇지?	You won't go to the library, _____?
4	그들은 내일 떠날 거야, 그렇지 않니?	They will leave tomorrow, _____?
5	나는 그 차를 사지 말아야 해, 그렇지?	I shouldn't buy the car, _____?

WRITING POINT ❸

• You don't like pizza, **do you**? 너는 피자를 싫어해 / 그렇지?

1	너는 형제가 있어, 그렇지 않니?	You have a brother, _____?
2	그는 영어를 가르쳐, 그렇지 않니?	He teaches English, _____?
3	그들은 서로 몰라, 그렇지?	They don't know each other, _____?
4	너는 이 근처에서 살았어, 그렇지 않니?	You lived near here, _____?
5	그들은 점심을 안 먹었어, 그렇지?	They didn't have lunch, _____?

우리말과 일치하도록 빈칸에 알맞은 말을 넣으시오.

• be동사의 부가의문문 •

1　넌 아직 준비가 안 됐어, 그렇지?

　　→ You are not ready yet, _____ _____?

2　그들은 런던에서 왔어, 그렇지 않니?

　　→ They are from London, _____ _____?

3　그녀의 머리는 길지 않았어, 그렇지?

　　→ Her hair wasn't long, _____ _____?

• 조동사의 부가의문문 •

4　그들은 그 기차를 탈 수 없어, 그렇지?

　　→ They can't catch the train, _____ _____?

5　너는 그는 저녁 식사에 초대할 거지, 그렇지 않니?

　　→ You will invite him to dinner, _____ _____?

6　우리는 지금 출발해야 해, 그렇지 않니?

　　→ We should start now, _____ _____?

• 일반동사의 부가의문문 •

7　너는 매운 음식을 좋아하지 않아, 그렇지?

　　→ You don't like spicy food, _____ _____?

8　그 슈퍼마켓은 자정에 문을 닫아, 그렇지 않니?

　　→ The supermarket closes at midnight, _____ _____?

9　그 바지는 너에게 맞지 않아, 그렇지?

　　→ The pants don't fit you, _____ _____?

10　그들은 어젯밤에 극장에 갔어, 그렇지 않니?

　　→ They went to the theater last night, _____ _____?

( ) 안의 말을 이용하여 우리말을 영어로 옮기시오.

1 너는 피곤하지 않지, 그렇지? (tired)

2 그녀는 자녀가 두 명이야, 그렇지 않니? (two children)

3 넌 불어를 못해, 그렇지? (can / French)

4 이 셔츠는 나에게 너무 커, 그렇지 않니? (too big / for me)

5 너는 대도시에 살아, 그렇지 않니? (a big city)

6 이 선생님은 너희 담임 선생님이었어, 그렇지 않니? (Mr. Lee / your homeroom teacher)

7 너는 그 비밀을 말하지 않을 거야, 그렇지? (will / tell the secret)

8 그들은 그 경기에서 이기지 못했어, 그렇지? (win the game)

9 그녀는 커피를 마시지 않아, 그렇지? (drink coffee)

10 그 안경은 네 것이야, 그렇지 않니? (the glasses / yours)

11 Jack, 네가 내 책을 빌려갔어, 그렇지 않니? (borrow)

12 너는 그 개를 돌봐줄 거지, 그렇지 않니? (will / take care of)

1 우리말과 같은 뜻이 되도록 빈칸에 알맞은 말을 쓰시오. (단, 명령문의 형태를 사용할 것)

(1) 네 휴대전화 전원을 꺼라.

→ _____ off your cell phone.

(2) 교실에서 뛰지 마라.

→ _____ _____ in the classroom.

(3) 학교에 지각하지 마라.

→ _____ _____ late for school.

2 (A)와 (B)에서 각각 한 표현씩을 골라 도서관에서 지켜야 할 규칙을 완성하시오.

(A)	(B)
Don't	quiet
Be	books
Return	take the books

(1) _____ in the library.

(2) _____ home.

(3) _____ on time.

3 그림을 보고 주어진 단어를 이용하여 감탄문을 만드시오.

→ _____ _____ _____
_____ _____! (How, tall, this)

4 다음 문장을 감탄문으로 바꾸어 쓰시오.

(1) You are very kind.

→ How _____ _____
_____!

(2) They are very beautiful flowers.

→ What _____ _____
_____ _____!

5 주어진 우리말을 참고하여 대화를 완성하시오.

A Tom doesn't like go shopping,
_____ _____? (그렇지?)
B No, he doesn't.

6 빈칸에 알맞은 부가의문문을 쓰시오.

(1) It isn't raining outside, _____
_____?

(2) You can help me today, _____
_____?

(3) He had a cold last week, _____
_____?

7 주어진 단어를 이용하여 우리말을 영작하시오.

(1) 이 책은 재미있어, 그렇지 않니? (interesting)

→ _____

(2) 너는 문을 잠그지 않았어, 그렇지? (lock)

→ _____

STEP 1 배운 문장을 쓰면서 외워보세요.

Score _____ / 15

Korean	English
1 그녀는 중학생이다.	_____ _____ a middle school student.
2 그것은 내 가방 안에 있다.	_____ _____ in my bag.
3 당신들은 좋은 이웃들이에요.	_____ _____ good neighbors.
4 그들은 자매이다.	_____ _____ sisters.
5 우리는 공항에 있다.	_____ _____ at the airport.
6 Tom과 나는 같은 반이다.	_____ _____ _____ _____ in the same class.
7 나는 피곤하고 졸리다.	_____ _____ _____ and _____.
8 내 생일은 4월이다.	_____ _____ _____ in April.
9 Rick과 나는 친한 친구이다.	_____ _____ _____ _____ close friends.
10 이 바지는 나에게 너무 크다.	_____ _____ _____ too big for me.
11 그녀는 사람들에게 예의 바르다.	_____ _____ _____ to people.
12 내가 가장 좋아하는 계절은 여름이다.	_____ _____ _____ _____ summer.
13 나의 형은 운동을 잘한다.	_____ _____ good at sports.
14 그 카페는 2층에 있다.	_____ _____ _____ on the second floor.
15 그들은 하와이에서 휴가 중이다.	_____ _____ on vacation in Hawaii.

STEP 2   배운 문장을 다시 한번 쓰면서 외워보세요.   Score _____ / 15

Korean	English
1 그녀는 중학생이다.	
2 그것은 내 가방 안에 있다.	
3 당신들은 좋은 이웃들이에요.	
4 그들은 자매이다.	
5 우리는 공항에 있다.	
6 Tom과 나는 같은 반이다.	
7 나는 피곤하고 졸리다.	
8 내 생일은 4월이다.	
9 Rick과 나는 친한 친구이다.	
10 이 바지는 나에게 너무 크다.	
11 그녀는 사람들에게 예의 바르다.	
12 내가 가장 좋아하는 계절은 여름이다.	
13 나의 형은 운동을 잘한다.	
14 그 카페는 2층에 있다.	The café
15 그들은 하와이에서 휴가 중이다.	

be동사의 부정문, 의문문

⬤ 월 ⬤ 일

STEP I 배운 문장을 쓰면서 외워보세요.

Score _____ / 15

Korean	English
1 나는 요리를 잘 못해.	_____ _____ _____ a good cook.
2 그녀는 그녀 방에 없다.	_____ _____ _____ in her room.
3 이 수프는 따뜻하지 않다.	_____ _____ _____ _____ warm.
4 저 신발은 내 것이 아니다.	_____ _____ _____ _____ mine.
5 그는 유명한 작가니?	_____ _____ a famous writer?
6 그들은 거실에 있나요?	_____ _____ in the living room?
7 나는 거짓말쟁이가 아니야.	_____ _____ _____ a liar.
8 오늘은 날씨가 춥지 않다.	The weather _____ _____ _____ today.
9 너는 음악에 관심이 있니?	_____ _____ interested in music?
10 너희 부모님은 엄격하시니?	_____ _____ _____ strict?
11 우리 갈 준비 되었어요?	_____ _____ ready to go?
12 이 채소들은 신선하지 않다.	_____ _____ _____ fresh.
13 우리는 지금 수업 중이 아니다.	_____ _____ _____ in class right now.
14 미나(Mina)와 민지(Minji)는 쌍둥이니?	_____ _____ _____ twins?
15 당신은 개들을 무서워하나요?	_____ _____ afraid of dogs?

STEP 2 배운 문장을 다시 한번 쓰면서 외워보세요. Score _____ / 15

Korean	English
1 나는 요리를 잘 못해.	
2 그녀는 그녀 방에 없다.	
3 이 수프는 따뜻하지 않다.	
4 저 신발은 내 것이 아니다.	Those
5 그는 유명한 작가니?	
6 그들은 거실에 있나요?	
7 나는 거짓말쟁이가 아니야.	
8 오늘은 날씨가 춥지 않다.	The weather
9 너는 음악에 관심이 있니?	
10 너희 부모님은 엄격하시니?	
11 우리 갈 준비 되었어요?	
12 이 채소들은 신선하지 않다.	
13 우리는 지금 수업 중이 아니다.	
14 미나(Mina)와 민지(Minji)는 쌍둥이니?	
15 당신은 개들을 무서워하나요?	

일반동사의 긍정문

STEP I 배운 문장을 쓰면서 외워보세요.

Score _____ / 15

	Korean	English
1	나는 매일 아침을 먹는다.	_____ _____ _____ every day.
2	그들은 저녁에 TV를 본다.	_____ _____ _____ in the evening.
3	그 학생들은 교복을 입는다.	_____ _____ _____ school uniforms.
4	그녀는 바이올린을 매일 연습한다.	_____ _____ the violin every day.
5	그는 버스로 학교에 간다.	_____ _____ _____ _____ by bus.
6	그녀는 학교에서 영어를 가르친다.	_____ _____ _____ at school.
7	내 여동생은 곱슬머리를 가지고 있다.	_____ _____ _____ curly hair.
8	우리는 주말마다 야외 스포츠를 즐긴다.	_____ _____ _____ _____ on weekends.
9	Greg와 Kelly는 방과 후 도서관에서 공부한다.	_____ _____ _____ _____ in the library after school.
10	요즘에는 많은 외국인들이 한국어를 배운다.	_____ _____ _____ these days.
11	그는 보통 점심으로 샌드위치를 먹는다.	_____ _____ _____ for lunch.
12	민수(Minsu)는 여가 시간에 만화책을 읽는다.	_____ _____ _____ in his free time.
13	Cathy는 매일 아침 머리를 감는다.	_____ _____ every morning.
14	그는 매일 그의 개를 산책시킨다.	_____ _____ _____ _____ every day.
15	그 새들은 매우 높이 난다.	_____ _____ _____ very high.

STEP 2   배운 문장을 다시 한번 쓰면서 외워보세요.   Score _____ / 15

Korean	English
1 나는 매일 아침을 먹는다.	
2 그들은 저녁에 TV를 본다.	
3 그 학생들은 교복을 입는다.	
4 그녀는 바이올린을 매일 연습한다.	
5 그는 버스로 학교에 간다.	
6 그녀는 학교에서 영어를 가르친다.	
7 내 여동생은 곱슬머리를 가지고 있다.	
8 우리는 주말마다 야외 스포츠를 즐긴다.	
9 Greg와 Kelly는 방과 후 도서관에서 공부한다.	
10 요즘에는 많은 외국인들이 한국어를 배운다.	Many
11 그는 보통 점심으로 샌드위치를 먹는다.	
12 민수(Minsu)는 여가 시간에 만화책을 읽는다.	
13 Cathy는 매일 아침 머리를 감는다.	
14 그는 매일 그의 개를 산책시킨다.	
15 그 새들은 매우 높이 난다.	The birds

일반동사의 부정문, 의문문

월 일

STEP I 배운 문장을 쓰면서 외워보세요.

Score _____ / 15

	Korean	English
1	나는 밤에는 공부하지 않는다.	_____ _____ _____ at night.
2	그녀는 커피를 마시지 않는다.	_____ _____ _____ coffee.
3	그 버스는 여기에 서지 않는다.	_____ _____ _____ _____ here.
4	너는 중국 음식을 좋아하니?	_____ _____ _____ Chinese food?
5	그는 드럼을 연주하니?	_____ _____ _____ the drums?
6	그들은 토요일에 일하니?	_____ _____ _____ on Saturday?
7	너희 아버지는 종종 요리를 하시니?	_____ _____ _____ often _____?
8	호주에는 눈이 내리지 않는다.	_____ _____ _____ in Australia.
9	우리에게는 시간이 많지 않다.	_____ _____ _____ much time.
10	그 식당은 아침을 제공하지 않는다.	_____ _____ _____ _____ breakfast.
11	나는 더운 날씨를 좋아하지 않는다.	_____ _____ _____ hot weather.
12	그 컴퓨터는 잘 작동하지 않는다.	_____ _____ _____ well.
13	이 버스는 공항까지 갑니까?	_____ _____ _____ to the airport?
14	John은 학교에 친구들이 많지 않다.	_____ _____ _____ many friends at school.
15	당신 나라의 사람들은 젓가락을 사용하나요?	_____ _____ in your country _____ chopsticks?

STEP 2 배운 문장을 다시 한번 쓰면서 외워보세요.   Score _____ / 15

	Korean	English
1	나는 밤에는 공부하지 않는다.	
2	그녀는 커피를 마시지 않는다.	
3	그 버스는 여기에 서지 않는다.	
4	너는 중국 음식을 좋아하니?	
5	그는 드럼을 연주하니?	Does
6	그들은 토요일에 일하니?	
7	너희 아버지는 종종 요리를 하시니?	
8	호주에는 눈이 내리지 않는다.	It
9	우리에게는 시간이 많지 않다.	We
10	그 식당은 아침을 제공하지 않는다.	
11	나는 더운 날씨를 좋아하지 않는다.	
12	그 컴퓨터는 잘 작동하지 않는다.	
13	이 버스는 공항까지 갑니까?	
14	John은 학교에 친구들이 많지 않다.	
15	당신 나라의 사람들은 젓가락을 사용하나요?	

STEP I 배운 문장을 쓰면서 외워보세요.

Score _____ / 15

	Korean	English
1	나는 어제 아팠다.	_____ _____ _____ yesterday.
2	나의 어머니는 간호사였다.	_____ _____ _____ a nurse.
3	우리는 오늘 아침 학교에 늦었다.	_____ _____ _____ for school this morning.
4	그는 2010년에 런던에 없었다.	_____ _____ _____ _____ in 2010.
5	그들은 피곤하지 않았다.	_____ _____ tired.
6	너는 지난 주말에 집에 있었니?	_____ _____ _____ last weekend?
7	그 호텔은 편안했니?	_____ _____ _____ comfortable?
8	내 여동생은 5월에 태어났다.	_____ _____ _____ in May.
9	프랑크푸르트는 독일의 수도였다.	Frankfurt _____ _____ _____ of Germany.
10	그들은 서로 친하지 않았다.	_____ _____ _____ to each other.
11	그 우산은 차 안에 없었다.	_____ _____ _____ in the car.
12	어젯밤 그 영화는 좋았니?	_____ _____ _____ good last night?
13	그 책은 내 침대 밑에 있었다.	_____ _____ _____ under my bed.
14	그것은 내 실수였어.	_____ _____ my mistake.
15	나의 부모님과 나는 지난 주에 휴가 중이었다.	_____ _____ _____ _____ _____ on vacation last week.

STEP 2 배운 문장을 다시 한번 쓰면서 외워보세요. Score _____ / 15

	Korean	English
1	나는 어제 아팠다.	
2	나의 어머니는 간호사였다.	
3	우리는 오늘 아침 학교에 늦었다.	
4	그는 2010년에 런던에 없었다.	
5	그들은 피곤하지 않았다.	
6	너는 지난 주말에 집에 있었니?	
7	그 호텔은 편안했니?	
8	내 여동생은 5월에 태어났다.	
9	프랑크푸르트는 독일의 수도였다.	Frankfurt
10	그들은 서로 친하지 않았다.	
11	그 우산은 차 안에 없었다.	
12	어젯밤 그 영화는 좋았니?	
13	그 책은 내 침대 밑에 있었다.	
14	그것은 내 실수였어.	It
15	나의 부모님과 나는 지난 주에 휴가 중이었다.	

일반동사의 과거형

STEP I　배운 문장을 쓰면서 외워보세요.

Score _____ / 15

	Korean	English
1	우리는 집에 일찍 갔다.	_____ _____ _____ early.
2	그는 그 시험에 합격했다.	_____ _____ the exam.
3	그녀는 그 음식을 먹지 않았다.	_____ _____ _____ the food.
4	우리는 그 소식을 듣지 않았다.	_____ _____ _____ the news.
5	너는 네 열쇠를 찾았니?	_____ _____ _____ your key?
6	그들은 그 경기에서 이겼니?	_____ _____ _____ the game?
7	우리는 지난 금요일에 영화를 보러 갔다.	_____ _____ _____ _____ last Friday.
8	Brown 씨는 우리를 저녁 식사에 초대했다.	Mr. Brown _____ _____ to dinner.
9	나는 내 가방을 버스에 두고 내렸다.	_____ _____ _____ _____ on the bus.
10	그들은 내 생일파티에 오지 않았다.	_____ _____ _____ to my birthday party.
11	내가 실수를 저질렀니?	_____ _____ _____ a mistake?
12	그들은 휴일을 즐겼니?	_____ _____ _____ their holiday?
13	그 기차는 정시에 도착하지 않았다.	_____ _____ _____ _____ on time.
14	Lisa는 미술 시간에 손가락을 베었다.	Lisa _____ _____ _____ in art class.
15	Steve는 어젯밤에 잠을 잘 자지 못했다.	Steve _____ _____ _____ last night.

STEP 2 배운 문장을 다시 한번 쓰면서 외워보세요.   Score _____ / 15

	Korean	English
1	우리는 집에 일찍 갔다.	
2	그는 그 시험에 합격했다.	
3	그녀는 그 음식을 먹지 않았다.	
4	우리는 그 소식을 듣지 않았다.	
5	너는 네 열쇠를 찾았니?	Did
6	그들은 그 경기에서 이겼니?	
7	우리는 지난 금요일에 영화를 보러 갔다.	
8	Brown 씨는 우리를 저녁 식사에 초대했다.	Mr. Brown
9	나는 내 가방을 버스에 두고 내렸다.	
10	그들은 내 생일파티에 오지 않았다.	
11	내가 실수를 저질렀니?	
12	그들은 휴일을 즐겼니?	
13	그 기차는 정시에 도착하지 않았다.	
14	Lisa는 미술 시간에 손가락을 베었다.	Lisa
15	Steve는 어젯밤에 잠을 잘 자지 못했다.	Steve

STEP I 배운 문장을 쓰면서 외워보세요.

Score _____ / 15

Korean	English
1 그들은 해변을 따라 걷고 있다.	_____ _____ _____ along the beach.
2 그 소녀는 벤치에 앉아 있다.	_____ _____ _____ _____ on the bench.
3 너는 안경을 쓰고 있지 않다.	_____ _____ _____ glasses.
4 너는 내 말을 듣고 있니?	_____ _____ _____ to me?
5 Kevin과 Lisa는 숙제를 하고 있니?	_____ _____ _____ _____ _____ their homework?
6 그 아이들은 길을 건너고 있다.	The children _____ _____ the street.
7 손님들은 그들의 코트를 벗고 있다.	The guests _____ _____ _____ their coats.
8 너는 나에게 진실을 말하고 있지 않아.	_____ _____ _____ me the truth.
9 그들은 지금 전화 통화 중이니?	_____ _____ _____ on the phone now?
10 그녀는 차 한잔을 마시고 있다.	_____ _____ _____ a cup of tea.
11 너는 너무 큰 소리로 노래 부르고 있어.	_____ _____ _____ too loudly.
12 그는 복사기를 사용 중이니?	_____ _____ _____ the copy machine?
13 너는 네 차 열쇠를 찾고 있니?	_____ _____ _____ _____ your car keys?
14 나의 할머니는 정원에서 꽃에 물을 주고 계신다.	My grandmother _____ _____ _____ _____ in the garden.
15 Tom과 Rachael은 통학 버스를 기다리고 있니?	_____ _____ _____ _____ _____ the school bus?

STEP 2 배운 문장을 다시 한번 쓰면서 외워보세요. Score _____ / 15

	Korean	English
1	그들은 해변을 따라 걷고 있다.	
2	그 소녀는 벤치에 앉아 있다.	
3	너는 안경을 쓰고 있지 않다.	
4	너는 내 말을 듣고 있니?	
5	Kevin과 Lisa는 숙제를 하고 있니?	
6	그 아이들은 길을 건너고 있다.	The children
7	손님들은 그들의 코트를 벗고 있다.	The guests
8	너는 나에게 진실을 말하고 있지 않아.	
9	그들은 지금 전화 통화 중이니?	
10	그녀는 차 한잔을 마시고 있다.	
11	너는 너무 큰 소리로 노래 부르고 있어.	
12	그는 복사기를 사용 중이니?	
13	너는 네 차 열쇠를 찾고 있니?	
14	나의 할머니는 정원에서 꽃에 물을 주고 계신다.	My grandmother
15	Tom과 Rachael은 통학 버스를 기다리고 있니?	

will, be going to

STEP I 배운 문장을 쓰면서 외워보세요.

	Korean	English
1	Eric은 우리를 역까지 차로 태워다 줄 것이다.	Eric _____ _____ _____ to the station.
2	나는 버스를 타지 않을 것이다. 걸어갈 것이다.	I _____ _____ _____ a bus. I _____ _____.
3	몇몇 사람들은 이것을 믿지 못할 것이다.	Some people _____ _____ _____ this.
4	너는 오늘 저녁에 집에 있을 거니?	_____ _____ _____ at home this evening?
5	나는 다음 달에 새 집으로 이사할 것이다.	I _____ _____ _____ _____ into a new house next month.
6	그는 내일 부산으로 떠날 것이다.	He _____ _____ _____ _____ _____ Busan tomorrow.
7	그들은 이번 주 토요일에 일할 거니?	_____ _____ _____ _____ _____ this Saturday?
8	나는 최선을 다 할 것이다.	I _____ _____ my best.
9	그들은 다음 달에 결혼 할 예정이다.	They _____ _____ _____ _____ next month.
10	너는 장래에 영화 감독이 될 거니?	_____ _____ _____ _____ in the future?
11	그의 아들은 다음달이면 열다섯 살이 된다.	His son _____ _____ _____ _____ next month.
12	너는 아무 문제 없을 거야.	You _____ _____ _____ any problems.
13	Ted는 7월에 비행기로 런던에 갈 것이다.	Ted _____ _____ _____ _____ to London in July.
14	나는 5분 후에 준비가 될 것이다.	I _____ _____ _____ in five minutes.
15	미래에, 사람들은 다른 행성으로 여행을 갈 것이다.	In the future, _____ _____ _____ to other planets.

STEP 2 배운 문장을 다시 한번 쓰면서 외워보세요. Score _____ / 15

Korean	English
1 Eric은 우리를 역까지 차로 태워다 줄 것이다.	Eric will
2 나는 버스를 타지 않을 것이다. 걸어갈 것이다.	I will
3 몇몇 사람들은 이것을 믿지 못할 것이다.	Some people will
4 너는 오늘 저녁에 집에 있을 거니?	Will
5 나는 다음 달에 새 집으로 이사할 것이다.	I am
6 그는 내일 부산으로 떠날 것이다.	He is
7 그들은 이번 주 토요일에 일할 거니?	Are they
8 나는 최선을 다 할 것이다.	I will
9 그들은 다음 달에 결혼 할 예정이다.	They are
10 너는 장래에 영화 감독이 될 거니?	Will you
11 그의 아들은 다음달이면 열다섯 살이 된다.	His son will
12 너는 아무 문제 없을 거야.	You will
13 Ted는 7월에 비행기로 런던에 갈 것이다.	Ted is
14 나는 5분 후에 준비가 될 것이다.	I will
15 미래에, 사람들은 다른 행성으로 여행을 갈 것이다.	In the future, people will

STEP I 배운 문장을 쓰면서 외워보세요.   Score _____ / 15

Korean	English
1 나는 바이올린을 연주할 수 있다.	_____ _____ _____ the violin.
2 그는 오늘 아픈지도 몰라.	_____ _____ _____ _____ today.
3 질문 하나 해도 될까요?	_____ _____ _____ a question?
4 우리는 물 없이 살 수 없다.	_____ _____ _____ without water.
5 내 숙제 좀 도와줄 수 있니?	_____ _____ _____ _____ with my homework?
6 Tom은 수영과 탁구를 아주 잘 할 수 있다.	Tom _____ _____ and _____ _____ _____ very well.
7 다음 주에는 눈이 올지도 모른다.	It _____ _____ next week.
8 그녀는 해산물을 좋아하지 않을 수도 있다.	She _____ _____ _____ seafood.
9 너는 도서관에 있는 컴퓨터들을 사용해도 좋다.	You _____ _____ _____ in the library.
10 제가 이 신발을 신어봐도 될까요?	_____ _____ try on these shoes?
11 어떤 사람들은 3개 국어를 할 수 있다.	_____ _____ _____ _____ three languages.
12 나의 할아버지는 안경 없이는 읽을 수 없다.	My grandfather _____ _____ without glasses.
13 나는 내 열쇠를 어디에서도 찾을 수가 없다.	I _____ _____ _____ _____ anywhere.
14 그는 100미터를 12초에 달릴 수 있다.	_____ _____ _____ 100 meters in 12 seconds.
15 네 지갑은 식탁 위에 있을 지도 모른다.	Your purse _____ _____ _____ _____ _____.

STEP 2   배운 문장을 다시 한번 쓰면서 외워보세요.   Score _____ / 15

	Korean	English
1	나는 바이올린을 연주할 수 있다.	
2	그는 오늘 아픈지도 몰라.	
3	질문 하나 해도 될까요?	May
4	우리는 물 없이 살 수 없다.	
5	내 숙제 좀 도와줄 수 있니?	Can you
6	Tom은 수영과 탁구를 아주 잘 할 수 있다.	Tom
7	다음 주에는 눈이 올지도 모른다.	It
8	그녀는 해산물을 좋아하지 않을 수도 있다.	
9	너는 도서관에 있는 컴퓨터들을 사용해도 좋다.	
10	제가 이 신발을 신어봐도 될까요?	
11	어떤 사람들은 3개 국어를 할 수 있다.	Some people
12	나의 할아버지는 안경 없이는 읽을 수 없다.	My grandfather
13	나는 내 열쇠를 어디에서도 찾을 수가 없다.	
14	그는 100미터를 12초에 달릴 수 있다.	
15	네 지갑은 식탁 위에 있을 지도 모른다.	Your purse

must, have to, should

STEP I 배운 문장을 쓰면서 외워보세요.

Score _____ / 15

	Korean	English
1	당신은 모든 질문에 답해야 합니다.	_____ must _____ all the questions.
2	학생들은 내일까지 숙제를 제출해야 한다.	_____ must hand in _____ _____ by _____.
3	Jane은 정크푸드를 너무 많이 먹으면 안 된다.	Jane must _____ _____ too much _____ _____.
4	그는 내일 아침 일찍 일어나야 한다.	_____ _____ _____ get up early tomorrow morning.
5	사과하실 필요 없습니다.	You _____ _____ _____ _____ sorry.
6	너는 규칙적으로 운동을 해야 한다.	You should _____ _____.
7	그는 너무 늦게까지 깨어있으면 안 된다.	He should _____ _____ _____ too late.
8	Jake는 그의 가족들과 더 많은 시간을 보내야 한다.	Jake should _____ _____ _____ with his family.
9	너는 네 약속을 지켜야 한다.	You must _____ _____ _____.
10	나는 오늘 내 숙제를 끝내야 한다.	I _____ _____ _____ my _____ today.
11	사람들은 공공장소에서 담배를 피우면 안 된다.	_____ must _____ _____ in public places.
12	너는 그것에 대해 걱정할 필요는 없다.	You _____ _____ _____ about it.
13	그들은 그 집을 사면 안 된다.	_____ should _____ _____ the house.
14	너는 수업 중에 네 휴대전화를 사용하면 안 된다.	You must _____ _____ _____ _____ during the class.
15	그들은 저녁 식사 값을 낼 필요가 없다.	They _____ _____ _____ for dinner

STEP 2 배운 문장을 다시 한번 쓰면서 외워보세요. Score _____ / 15

	Korean	English
1	당신은 모든 질문에 답해야 합니다.	You must
2	학생들은 내일까지 숙제를 제출해야 한다.	Students must
3	Jane은 정크푸드를 너무 많이 먹으면 안 된다.	Jane must
4	그는 내일 아침 일찍 일어나야 한다.	He has
5	사과하실 필요 없습니다.	
6	너는 규칙적으로 운동을 해야 한다.	You should
7	그는 너무 늦게까지 깨어있으면 안 된다.	He should
8	Jake는 그의 가족들과 더 많은 시간을 보내야 한다.	Jake should
9	너는 네 약속을 지켜야 한다.	You must
10	나는 오늘 내 숙제를 끝내야 한다.	I have
11	사람들은 공공장소에서 담배를 피우면 안 된다.	People must
12	너는 그것에 대해 걱정할 필요는 없다.	
13	그들은 그 집을 사면 안 된다.	They should
14	너는 수업 중에 네 휴대전화를 사용하면 안 된다.	You must
15	그들은 저녁 식사 값을 낼 필요가 없다.	

STEP 1   배운 문장을 쓰면서 외워보세요.   Score _____ / 15

	Korean	English
1	Jane의 생일이 언제야?	_____ _____ Jane's birthday?
2	너는 어디 출신이니?	_____ _____ _____ from?
3	그는 언제 테니스를 연습하니?	_____ _____ _____ _____ tennis?
4	너는 어디에서 옷을 사니?	_____ _____ _____ _____ your clothes?
5	그녀는 언제 너에게 전화했니?	_____ _____ _____ _____ you?
6	그는 어디에 그의 우산을 두고 왔니?	_____ _____ _____ _____ his umbrella?
7	너는 학교 끝나고 어디에 있었니?	_____ _____ _____ after school?
8	영화는 언제 시작하니?	_____ _____ the movie _____?
9	다음 버스는 언제 도착하나요?	_____ _____ the next bus _____?
10	너는 네 선글라스를 언제 잃어버렸니?	_____ _____ _____ _____ your sunglasses?
11	코알라들은 어디에 사나요?	_____ _____ koalas _____?
12	가장 가까운 버스 정류장이 어디죠?	_____ _____ the nearest bus _____?
13	너는 언제 일본을 여행했니?	_____ _____ _____ _____ to Japan?
14	그 사고는 언제 일어난 거죠?	_____ _____ the accident _____?
15	실종된 아이는 어디에 있었나요?	_____ _____ the missing child?

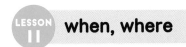
STEP 2 배운 문장을 다시 한번 쓰면서 외워보세요.   Score _____ / 15

Korean	English
1 Jane의 생일이 언제야?	
2 너는 어디 출신이니?	
3 그는 언제 테니스를 연습하니?	
4 너는 어디에서 옷을 사니?	
5 그녀는 언제 너에게 전화했니?	
6 그는 어디에 그의 우산을 두고 왔니?	
7 너는 학교 끝나고 어디에 있었니?	
8 영화는 언제 시작하니?	When does
9 다음 버스는 언제 도착하나요?	When does
10 너는 네 선글라스를 언제 잃어버렸니?	
11 코알라들은 어디에 사나요?	
12 가장 가까운 버스 정류장이 어디죠?	
13 너는 언제 일본을 여행했니?	
14 그 사고는 언제 일어난 거죠?	
15 실종된 아이는 어디에 있었나요?	

who, what

STEP I 배운 문장을 쓰면서 외워보세요.

Score _____ / 15

Korean	English
1 그의 차는 무슨 색이니?	_____ _____ _____ his car?
2 너는 누구와 함께 일하니?	_____ _____ _____ work with?
3 상자 안에 무엇이 있니?	_____ _____ in the box?
4 그에게 무슨 일이 일어났니?	_____ _____ to him?
5 그는 파티에 누구를 초대했니?	_____ _____ _____ _____ to the party?
6 이 단어는 무슨 뜻이니?	_____ _____ this word _____?
7 너는 보통 몇 시에 자러 가니?	_____ _____ _____ _____ usually go to bed?
8 누가 소파에 앉아있니?	_____ _____ _____ on the sofa?
9 누가 어제 그의 지갑을 훔쳤니?	_____ _____ his wallet yesterday?
10 부엌에 누가 있니?	_____ in the kitchen?
11 당신의 가장 큰 실수는 무엇이었나요?	_____ _____ your biggest mistake?
12 누가 알람을 껐니?	_____ _____ _____ the alarm?
13 너는 보통 여가 시간에 뭘 하니?	_____ _____ _____ usually _____ in your free time?
14 당신은 누구를 가장 존경합니까?	_____ _____ _____ respect the most?
15 너는 생일 선물로 뭘 원하니?	_____ _____ _____ _____ for your birthday?

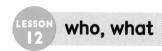 **who, what**

STEP 2 배운 문장을 다시 한번 쓰면서 외워보세요. Score _____ / 15

Korean	English
1 그의 차는 무슨 색이니?	
2 너는 누구와 함께 일하니?	Who
3 상자 안에 무엇이 있니?	
4 그에게 무슨 일이 일어났니?	
5 그는 파티에 누구를 초대했니?	
6 이 단어는 무슨 뜻이니?	What
7 너는 보통 몇 시에 자러 가니?	
8 누가 소파에 앉아있니?	
9 누가 어제 그의 지갑을 훔쳤니?	
10 부엌에 누가 있니?	
11 당신의 가장 큰 실수는 무엇이었나요?	
12 누가 알람을 껐니?	
13 너는 보통 여가 시간에 뭘 하니?	
14 당신은 누구를 가장 존경합니까?	
15 너는 생일 선물로 뭘 원하니?	

STEP 1   배운 문장을 쓰면서 외워보세요.

Score _____ / 15

Korean	English
1 그녀는 왜 그렇게 기분이 좋니?	_____ _____ _____ so happy?
2 그 아이들은 왜 웃고 있니?	_____ _____ the children _____?
3 네 크리스마스는 어땠니?	_____ _____ your Christmas?
4 그들은 서로 어떻게 만났니?	_____ _____ _____ _____ each other?
5 그는 왜 회의에 늦었니?	_____ _____ _____ _____ for the meeting?
6 스페인 여행은 어땠니?	_____ _____ _____ _____ to Spain?
7 이 기계는 어떻게 작동하니?	_____ _____ this machine _____?
8 너는 조부모님을 얼마나 자주 찾아 뵙니?	_____ _____ _____ _____ _____ your grandparents?
9 너는 한 달에 외식을 몇 번 하니?	_____ _____ _____ _____ _____ eat out a month?
10 너희 학교는 여기서 얼마나 머니?	_____ _____ _____ your school from here?
11 당신 나라의 날씨는 어떻습니까?	_____ _____ _____ _____ in your country?
12 네 수학 시험은 어땠니?	_____ _____ your math test?
13 당신 이름의 철자가 어떻게 되죠?	_____ _____ you _____ your name?
14 너는 왜 이렇게 서두르니?	_____ _____ _____ in a hurry?
15 표가 몇 장이나 필요하세요?	_____ _____ do you need?

STEP 2   배운 문장을 다시 한번 쓰면서 외워보세요.   Score _____ / 15

	Korean	English
1	그녀는 왜 그렇게 기분이 좋니?	
2	그 아이들은 왜 웃고 있니?	
3	네 크리스마스는 어땠니?	
4	그들은 서로 어떻게 만났니?	
5	그는 왜 회의에 늦었니?	
6	스페인 여행은 어땠니?	
7	이 기계는 어떻게 작동하니?	
8	너는 조부모님을 얼마나 자주 찾아 뵙니?	
9	너는 한 달에 외식을 몇 번 하니?	How many
10	너희 학교는 여기서 얼마나 머니?	How
11	당신 나라의 날씨는 어떻습니까?	How
12	네 수학 시험은 어땠니?	
13	당신 이름의 철자가 어떻게 되죠?	How do
14	너는 왜 이렇게 서두르니?	
15	표가 몇 장이나 필요하세요?	

There is/are, 비인칭 주어 it

STEP 1   배운 문장을 쓰면서 외워보세요.

Score _____ / 15

Korean	English
1 오늘은 내 생일이다.	_____ _____ my birthday today.
2 지금 몇 시니?	What time _____ _____ now?
3 오늘이 무슨 요일이니?	_____ _____ _____ _____ today?
4 정원에 큰 나무 한 그루가 있다.	_____ _____ _____ _____ _____ in the garden.
5 우리 반에는 30명의 학생들이 있다.	_____ _____ thirty _____ in our class.
6 잔에 물이 전혀 없다.	_____ _____ any _____ in the glass.
7 이 근처에 주차장이 있나요?	_____ _____ a parking lot _____ _____ ?
8 식구가 몇 명이나 되나요?	How many _____ _____ _____ in your family?
9 이 안은 매우 덥다.	_____ _____ very _____ in here.
10 밖에 비가 오고 있니?	_____ _____ raining outside?
11 어제는 따뜻하고 화창했다.	_____ _____ _____ and _____ yesterday.
12 1년에는 사계절이 있다.	_____ _____ _____ in a year.
13 그 정원에는 꽃이 많지 않다.	_____ _____ many _____ in the garden.
14 오늘 저녁에 공원에서 콘서트가 있다.	_____ _____ _____ _____ in the park this evening.
15 자전거로 10분 걸려요.	_____ _____ 10 minutes by bike.

STEP 2   배운 문장을 다시 한번 쓰면서 외워보세요.   Score _____ / 15

	Korean	English
1	오늘은 내 생일이다.	It
2	지금 몇 시니?	What
3	오늘이 무슨 요일이니?	What
4	정원에 큰 나무 한 그루가 있다.	There
5	우리 반에는 30명의 학생들이 있다.	There
6	잔에 물이 전혀 없다.	There isn't
7	이 근처에 주차장이 있나요?	Is
8	식구가 몇 명이나 되나요?	How
9	이 안은 매우 덥다.	It
10	밖에 비가 오고 있니?	Is
11	어제는 따뜻하고 화창했다.	It
12	1년에는 사계절이 있다.	There
13	그 정원에는 꽃이 많지 않다.	There
14	오늘 저녁에 공원에서 콘서트가 있다.	There
15	자전거로 10분 걸려요.	It

감각동사＋형용사

월 ○ 일

STEP I 배운 문장을 쓰면서 외워보세요.

Score _____ / 15

	Korean	English
1	너는 오늘 피곤해 보인다.	You _____ _____ today.
2	그녀의 목소리는 아름답게 들린다.	Her voice _____ _____ .
3	그 채소들은 신선해 보이지 않는다.	The vegetables _____ _____ _____ .
4	그것은 맛이 좋으니?	_____ it _____ _____ ?
5	이 그림은 사진처럼 보인다.	This picture _____ _____ a photo.
6	그것은 좋은 계획처럼 들린다.	It _____ _____ a good plan.
7	그는 어떻게 생겼어?	What does he _____ _____ ?
8	이 약은 맛이 쓰다.	This medicine _____ _____ .
9	이 소파는 편안하게 느껴진다.	This sofa _____ _____ .
10	이 샴푸는 장미 냄새가 난다.	This shampoo _____ _____ _____ .
11	이 아이스크림은 녹차 맛이 난다.	This ice cream _____ _____ _____ _____ .
12	그의 설명은 어렵게 들린다.	His explanation _____ _____ .
13	나는 네가 없으면 외롭게 느껴져.	_____ _____ _____ without you.
14	나는 가끔 천재처럼 느껴진다.	I sometimes _____ _____ a genius.
15	Dave는 연설하기 전에 초조함을 느꼈다.	Dave _____ _____ before the speech.

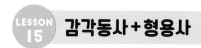

STEP 2   배운 문장을 다시 한번 쓰면서 외워보세요.   Score _____ / 15

	Korean	English
1	너는 오늘 피곤해 보인다.	
2	그녀의 목소리는 아름답게 들린다.	
3	그 채소들은 신선해 보이지 않는다.	The vegetables
4	그것은 맛이 좋으니?	Does it
5	이 그림은 사진처럼 보인다.	This picture
6	그것은 좋은 계획처럼 들린다.	It
7	그는 어떻게 생겼어?	What
8	이 약은 맛이 쓰다.	
9	이 소파는 편안하게 느껴진다.	
10	이 샴푸는 장미 냄새가 난다.	
11	이 아이스크림은 녹차 맛이 난다.	
12	그의 설명은 어렵게 들린다.	
13	나는 네가 없으면 외롭게 느껴져.	
14	나는 가끔 천재처럼 느껴진다.	I sometimes
15	Dave는 연설하기 전에 초조함을 느꼈다.	Dave

수여동사

 월 ◯ 일

	Korean	English
1	나는 Mike에게 이메일을 썼다.	I wrote _____ _____ _____.
2	그는 나에게 사진 한 장을 보여주었다.	He showed _____ _____ _____.
3	김 선생님은 우리에게 수학을 가르치신다.	Mr. Kim teaches _____ _____.
4	그는 우리에게 피자를 만들어주었다.	He made _____ _____.
5	그는 나에게 질문을 하나 했다.	He asked _____ _____ _____.
6	나는 내 남동생에게 장난감 자동차를 사주었다.	I bought a toy car _____ _____ _____.
7	그들은 항상 서로에게 진실을 말한다.	They always _____ _____ _____ to each other.
8	Frank는 우리에게 재미있는 이야기를 하나 해주었다.	Frank told _____ _____ _____ _____.
9	그 여행은 나에게 특별한 경험을 주었다.	The trip gave _____ _____ _____ _____.
10	나의 삼촌은 내 생일에 나에게 선물을 보내주었다.	My uncle _____ _____ _____ _____ on my birthday.
11	아빠는 일주일에 한 번 우리에게 저녁을 요리해주신다.	My dad _____ _____ _____ once a week.
12	Linda는 나에게 멋진 모자를 만들어주었다.	Linda _____ a nice hat _____ _____.
13	Steve는 그의 차를 누구에게도 빌려주지 않는다.	Steve _____ _____ his car _____ anyone.
14	Mindy는 나에게 한자를 몇 자 가르쳐주었다.	Mindy _____ some _____ _____ _____ _____.
15	그는 그의 딸에게 강아지 한 마리를 사 주었다.	He _____ a puppy _____ _____ _____.

STEP 2 배운 문장을 다시 한번 쓰면서 외워보세요. Score _____ / 15

	Korean	English
1	나는 Mike에게 이메일을 썼다.	I wrote Mike
2	그는 나에게 사진 한 장을 보여주었다.	He showed me
3	김 선생님은 우리에게 수학을 가르치신다.	Mr. Kim teaches us
4	그는 우리에게 피자를 만들어주었다.	He made us
5	그는 나에게 질문을 하나 했다.	He asked me
6	나는 내 남동생에게 장난감 자동차를 사주었다.	I bought a
7	그들은 항상 서로에게 진실을 말한다.	They always tell the
8	Frank는 우리에게 재미있는 이야기를 하나 해주었다.	Frank told us
9	그 여행은 나에게 특별한 경험을 주었다.	The trip gave me
10	나의 삼촌은 내 생일에 나에게 선물을 보내주었다.	My uncle sent me
11	아빠는 일주일에 한 번 우리에게 저녁을 요리해주신다.	My dad cooks us
12	Linda는 나에게 멋진 모자를 만들어주었다.	Linda made a
13	Steve는 그의 차를 누구에게도 빌려주지 않는다.	Steve doesn't lend his
14	Mindy는 나에게 한자를 몇 자 가르쳐주었다.	Mindy taught some
15	그는 그의 딸에게 강아지 한 마리를 사주었다.	He bought a

to부정사의 명사적 용법

STEP I   배운 문장을 쓰면서 외워보세요.   Score _____ / 15

	Korean	English
1	외국어를 배우는 것은 유용하다.	It _____ _____ _____ _____ a foreign language.
2	캠핑을 가는 것은 재미있다.	It _____ _____ _____ _____ camping.
3	내 취미는 소설을 읽는 것이다.	My hobby _____ _____ _____ novels.
4	나는 전 세계를 여행하기를 원한다.	I _____ _____ _____ around the world.
5	서울에 사는 것은 절대 지루하지 않다.	It _____ never boring _____ _____ in Seoul.
6	야채를 먹는 것은 건강에 좋다.	It _____ _____ _____ _____ vegetables.
7	그의 꿈은 대통령이 되는 것이다.	His dream _____ _____ _____ president.
8	Jim과 Sue는 함께 시간 보내기를 원한다.	Jim and Sue _____ _____ _____ _____ together.
9	Mary는 사진 찍는 것을 좋아한다.	Mary _____ _____ _____ pictures.
10	당신은 왜 가수가 되기로 결심했나요?	Why _____ you _____ _____ _____ a singer?
11	아침 6시에 일어나는 것은 쉽지 않다.	It is _____ _____ _____ get up at 6 in the morning.
12	내 숙제는 나의 특별한 재능에 대해서 글을 쓰는 것이다.	My homework _____ _____ _____ about my special talent.
13	그 일을 내일까지 끝내는 것은 불가능하다.	It is impossible _____ _____ _____ _____ by tomorrow.
14	우리는 이번 주말에 양로원을 방문할 계획이다.	We _____ _____ _____ the nursing home this weekend.
15	그 수학 문제를 푸는 것은 매우 쉬웠다.	_____ _____ very easy _____ _____ the math problem.

STEP 2 배운 문장을 다시 한번 쓰면서 외워보세요.

Score _____ / 15

	Korean	English
1	외국어를 배우는 것은 유용하다.	It
2	캠핑을 가는 것은 재미있다.	It
3	내 취미는 소설을 읽는 것이다.	My hobby
4	나는 전 세계를 여행하기를 원한다.	I want
5	서울에 사는 것은 절대 지루하지 않다.	It
6	야채를 먹는 것은 건강에 좋다.	It
7	그의 꿈은 대통령이 되는 것이다.	His dream
8	Jim과 Sue는 함께 시간 보내기를 원한다.	
9	Mary는 사진 찍는 것을 좋아한다.	
10	당신은 왜 가수가 되기로 결심했나요?	Why did
11	아침 6시에 일어나는 것은 쉽지 않다.	It
12	내 숙제는 나의 특별한 재능에 대해서 글을 쓰는 것이다.	My homework
13	그 일을 내일까지 끝내는 것은 불가능하다.	It
14	우리는 이번 주말에 양로원을 방문할 계획이다.	We plan
15	그 수학 문제를 푸는 것은 매우 쉬웠다.	It

to부정사의 형용사적, 부사적 용법

월 일

STEP I 배운 문장을 쓰면서 외워보세요.

Score _____ / 15

	Korean	English
1	너는 밤에 입을 재킷이 필요하다.	You need _____ _____ _____ _____ at night.
2	그는 그를 도와줄 친구들이 많다.	He has _____ _____ _____ _____ _____ .
3	한국에는 방문할 곳이 많이 있다.	There are _____ _____ _____ _____ in Korea.
4	사람들은 건강을 유지하기 위해 운동한다.	People exercise _____ _____ _____ _____ .
5	나는 공부하기 위해 도서관에 갔다.	I went to the library _____ _____ .
6	그는 음악을 듣기 위해 라디오를 켰다.	He turned on the radio _____ _____ _____ _____ .
7	모든 사람은 사랑할 누군가가 필요하다.	Everyone needs _____ _____ _____ .
8	나는 이번 주에 해야 할 숙제가 많다.	I have a lot of _____ _____ _____ this week.
9	그들은 살 집을 찾고 있다.	They are looking for _____ _____ _____ _____ _____ .
10	그는 살을 빼기 위해 매일 아침 조깅하러 간다.	He goes jogging every morning _____ _____ _____ .
11	나는 개를 산책시키기 위해 공원에 갔다.	I went to the park _____ _____ _____ _____ .
12	점심 먹을 시간이다.	It is _____ _____ _____ _____ .
13	그는 대기오염을 줄이기 위한 방법을 소개했다.	He introduced a way _____ _____ _____ _____ .
14	민수(Minsu)는 좋은 성적을 받기 위해 밤새 공부했다.	Minsu studied all night _____ _____ _____ _____ .
15	너는 쓸 펜이 있니?	Do you have _____ _____ _____ _____ ?

STEP 2 배운 문장을 다시 한번 쓰면서 외워보세요. Score _____ / 15

	Korean	English
1	너는 밤에 입을 재킷이 필요하다.	
2	그는 그를 도와줄 친구들이 많다.	He has many
3	한국에는 방문할 곳이 많이 있다.	There
4	사람들은 건강을 유지하기 위해 운동한다.	People
5	나는 공부하기 위해 도서관에 갔다.	
6	그는 음악을 듣기 위해 라디오를 켰다.	He
7	모든 사람은 사랑할 누군가가 필요하다.	Everyone
8	나는 이번 주에 해야 할 숙제가 많다.	I
9	그들은 살 집을 찾고 있다.	
10	그는 살을 빼기 위해 매일 아침 조깅하러 간다.	He
11	나는 개를 산책시키기 위해 공원에 갔다.	
12	점심 먹을 시간이다.	It is
13	그는 대기오염을 줄이기 위한 방법을 소개했다.	
14	민수(Minsu)는 좋은 성적을 받기 위해 밤새 공부했다.	
15	너는 쓸 펜이 있니?	Do

STEP I 배운 문장을 쓰면서 외워보세요.

Score _____ / 15

Korean	English
1 빗속을 운전하는 것은 위험하다.	_____ in the rain _____ dangerous.
2 하루 종일 집에 있는 것은 지루하다.	_____ _____ _____ all day _____ boring.
3 매일 운동하는 것은 쉽지 않다.	_____ every day _____ _____ easy.
4 충분한 물을 마시는 것은 너에게 좋다.	_____ _____ _____ _____ _____ good for you.
5 내가 가장 좋아하는 것은 농구하는 것이다.	My favorite thing is _____ _____.
6 나는 영화 보는 것을 즐긴다.	I _____ _____ movies.
7 그들은 숙제 하는 것을 끝냈다.	They _____ _____ their _____.
8 쉽게 포기하는 것은 나쁜 습관이다.	_____ _____ _____ is a bad habit.
9 집을 짓는 것은 많은 시간이 필요하다.	_____ _____ _____ takes a lot of time.
10 그의 성공 비결은 늘 최선을 다하는 것이다.	His secret to success is always _____ _____ _____.
11 그녀의 직업은 아픈 사람들을 돕는 것이다.	_____ _____ _____ _____ sick people.
12 나는 가끔씩 혼자 있는 것을 즐긴다.	I sometimes _____ _____ _____.
13 그들은 수업 중에 계속 떠들었다.	They _____ _____ during the class.
14 내 목표는 수학에서 좋은 점수를 얻는 것이다.	_____ _____ _____ _____ a good score in math.
15 너는 너무 많은 정크푸드를 먹는 것을 피해야 한다.	You should _____ _____ too much _____ _____.

STEP 2   배운 문장을 다시 한번 쓰면서 외워보세요.   Score _____ / 15

	Korean	English
1	빗속을 운전하는 것은 위험하다.	
2	하루 종일 집에 있는 것은 지루하다.	
3	매일 운동하는 것은 쉽지 않다.	
4	충분한 물을 마시는 것은 너에게 좋다.	
5	내가 가장 좋아하는 것은 농구하는 것이다.	My favorite thing
6	나는 영화 보는 것을 즐긴다.	
7	그들은 숙제 하는 것을 끝냈다.	They finished
8	쉽게 포기하는 것은 나쁜 습관이다.	
9	집을 짓는 것은 많은 시간이 필요하다.	
10	그의 성공 비결은 늘 최선을 다하는 것이다.	His secret
11	그녀의 직업은 아픈 사람들을 돕는 것이다.	Her job
12	나는 가끔씩 혼자 있는 것을 즐긴다.	I
13	그들은 수업 중에 계속 떠들었다.	They
14	내 목표는 수학에서 좋은 점수를 얻는 것이다.	My goal
15	너는 너무 많은 정크푸드를 먹는 것을 피해야 한다.	You should

수량 형용사, 빈도부사

월 일

STEP I 배운 문장을 쓰면서 외워보세요.

Score _____ / 15

Korean	English
1 그 도서관에는 책이 많이 있니?	_____ _____ _____ _____ in the library?
2 그는 커피를 많이 마시지 않는다.	He doesn't _____ _____ _____.
3 그들은 많은 질문들을 했다.	They asked _____ _____ _____ _____.
4 우리는 많은 음식을 샀다.	We bought _____ _____ _____ _____.
5 나는 보통 걸어서 학교에 간다.	_____ _____ _____ to school.
6 너는 자주 운동을 하니?	_____ you _____ _____?
7 나는 절대로 그를 다시 보지 않을 거야.	I _____ _____ _____ him again.
8 우리는 해결해야 할 문제들이 많이 있다.	We have _____ _____ _____ _____ to solve.
9 런던은 종종 날씨가 흐리다.	It _____ _____ _____ in London.
10 너는 단것을 너무 많이 먹으면 안 된다.	You should not eat _____ _____ _____.
11 우리에게는 그 일을 끝낼 시간이 많지 않다.	We don't have _____ _____ _____ _____ the work.
12 나는 그 축제에서 많은 외국인들을 만났다.	I met _____ _____ _____ _____ at the festival.
13 나의 아버지는 직장에서 늘 바쁘시다.	My father _____ _____ _____ at work.
14 그녀는 옷에 너무 많은 돈을 쓴다.	She spends _____ _____ _____ on clothes.
15 너는 언제든지 나에게 도움을 청해도 돼.	You _____ _____ _____ _____ for help.

STEP 2   배운 문장을 다시 한번 쓰면서 외워보세요.   Score _____ / 15

	Korean	English
1	그 도서관에는 책이 많이 있니?	Are there
2	그는 커피를 많이 마시지 않는다.	
3	그들은 많은 질문들을 했다.	
4	우리는 많은 음식을 샀다.	
5	나는 보통 걸어서 학교에 간다.	
6	너는 자주 운동을 하니?	
7	나는 절대로 그를 다시 보지 않을 거야.	I will
8	우리는 해결해야 할 문제들이 많이 있다.	We
9	런던은 종종 날씨가 흐리다.	It
10	너는 단것을 너무 많이 먹으면 안 된다.	You should not
11	우리에게는 그 일을 끝낼 시간이 많지 않다.	We
12	나는 그 축제에서 많은 외국인들을 만났다.	
13	나의 아버지는 직장에서 늘 바쁘시다.	
14	그녀는 옷에 너무 많은 돈을 쓴다.	
15	너는 언제든지 나에게 도움을 청해도 돼.	

비교급, 최상급

STEP I 배운 문장을 쓰면서 외워보세요.

	Korean	English
1	내 가방은 네 것보다 더 무겁다.	My bag _____ _____ _____ yours.
2	나에게, 영어는 수학보다 더 쉽다.	For me, English _____ _____ _____ math.
3	Sally는 셋 중 가장 어리다.	Sally is _____ of _____ _____.
4	나일강은 세계에서 가장 긴 강이다.	The Nile is _____ _____ _____ in the world.
5	상어는 바다에서 가장 위험한 동물이다.	Sharks are _____ _____ _____ _____ in the sea.
6	망고는 오렌지보다 더 달다.	Mangos _____ _____ _____ oranges.
7	백설공주는 그 마녀보다 더 아름답다.	Snow White is _____ _____ _____ the witch.
8	그 반에는 여자 아이가 남자 아이보다 더 많다.	There are _____ _____ _____ _____ in the class.
9	오늘은 내 인생에서 가장 행복한 날이다.	Today is _____ _____ _____ in my life.
10	이곳은 마을에서 가장 저렴한 식당이다.	This is _____ _____ _____ in the town.
11	그는 세계에서 가장 빨리 달리는 사람이다.	He is _____ _____ _____ in the world.
12	거북이는 다른 동물들보다 더 오래 산다.	Turtles _____ _____ _____ other animals.
13	세계에서 가장 높은 산은 어디입니까?	What _____ _____ _____ _____ in the world?
14	아이스하키는 캐나다에서 가장 인기 있는 스포츠이다.	Ice hockey is _____ _____ _____ _____ in Canada.
15	네 인생에서 가장 중요한 것은 무엇이니?	What _____ _____ _____ _____ _____ in your life?

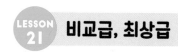

STEP 2   배운 문장을 다시 한번 쓰면서 외워보세요.

Score _____ / 15

	Korean	English
1	내 가방은 네 것보다 더 무겁다.	
2	나에게, 영어는 수학보다 더 쉽다.	For me,
3	Sally는 셋 중 가장 어리다.	Sally
4	나일강은 세계에서 가장 긴 강이다.	The Nile is
5	상어는 바다에서 가장 위험한 동물이다.	Sharks
6	망고는 오렌지보다 더 달다.	Mangos
7	백설공주는 그 마녀보다 더 아름답다.	Snow White
8	그 반에는 여자 아이가 남자 아이보다 더 많다.	There are
9	오늘은 내 인생에서 가장 행복한 날이다.	Today is
10	이곳은 마을에서 가장 저렴한 식당이다.	This is
11	그는 세계에서 가장 빨리 달리는 사람이다.	He is
12	거북이는 다른 동물들보다 더 오래 산다.	Turtles
13	세계에서 가장 높은 산은 어디입니까?	
14	아이스하키는 캐나다에서 가장 인기 있는 스포츠이다.	Ice hockey is
15	네 인생에서 가장 중요한 것은 무엇이니?	

STEP I 배운 문장을 쓰면서 외워보세요.

Score _____ / 15

Korean	English
1 이 침대는 돌처럼 딱딱하다.	This bed _____ _____ _____ _____ a rock.
2 그녀의 피부는 눈처럼 하얗다.	Her skin _____ _____ _____ _____ snow.
3 그 물은 얼음처럼 차갑다.	The water _____ _____ _____ _____ ice.
4 Jane은 Jim만큼 테니스를 잘 친다.	Jane plays tennis _____ _____ _____ Jim.
5 내 머리는 너의 것만큼 길지 않다.	My hair is _____ _____ _____ _____ yours.
6 달은 태양만큼 밝지 않다.	The moon is _____ _____ _____ _____ the sun.
7 올 여름은 작년 여름만큼 덥지 않다.	This summer is _____ _____ _____ _____ last summer.
8 그의 아이디어는 네 것만큼 좋지 않다.	His idea is _____ _____ _____ _____ yours.
9 John은 Mark만큼 열심히 일하지 않는다.	John works _____ _____ _____ Mark.
10 Bill은 그의 아버지만큼 키가 크다.	Bill _____ _____ _____ _____ his father.
11 이 새로 산 소파는 예전 것만큼 편하다.	This new sofa _____ _____ _____ _____ the old one.
12 돈은 건강만큼 중요하지 않다.	Money is _____ _____ _____ _____ good health.
13 나는 너만큼 높이 뛸 수 있다.	I can jump _____ _____ _____ you.
14 그는 그가 할 수 있는 만큼 빨리 달리고 있다.	He is running _____ _____ _____ _____ _____.
15 나는 TV를 너만큼 많이 보지 않는다.	I do not watch TV _____ _____ _____ you.

STEP 2　배운 문장을 다시 한번 쓰면서 외워보세요.　　　　　　　　　　Score _____ / 15

	Korean	English
1	이 침대는 돌처럼 딱딱하다.	
2	그녀의 피부는 눈처럼 하얗다.	
3	그 물은 얼음처럼 차갑다.	The water
4	Jane은 Jim만큼 테니스를 잘 친다.	
5	내 머리는 너의 것만큼 길지 않다.	My hair
6	달은 태양만큼 밝지 않다.	The moon
7	올 여름은 작년 여름만큼 덥지 않다.	This summer
8	그의 아이디어는 네 것만큼 좋지 않다.	
9	John은 Mark만큼 열심히 일하지 않는다.	
10	Bill은 그의 아버지만큼 키가 크다.	
11	이 새로 산 소파는 예전 것만큼 편하다.	This new sofa
12	돈은 건강만큼 중요하지 않다.	
13	나는 너만큼 높이 뛸 수 있다.	I can
14	그는 그가 할 수 있는 만큼 빨리 달리고 있다.	
15	나는 TV를 너만큼 많이 보지 않는다.	

STEP I 배운 문장을 쓰면서 외워보세요. Score _____ / 15

Korean	English
1 우리는 정오에 점심을 먹는다.	We have lunch _____ _____.
2 그 공연은 8월 24일에 있다.	The concert is _____ _____ _____.
3 그는 2010년에 서울로 이사 갔다.	They moved to Seoul _____ _____.
4 그녀는 버스 정류장에 서있다.	She is standing _____ _____ _____ _____.
5 한 남자가 내 옆에 앉았다.	A man sat _____ _____ _____.
6 밤에 혼자 걷는 것은 위험하다.	It is dangerous to walk alone _____ _____.
7 나는 거실 소파 위에서 너의 노트북을 봤어.	I saw your laptop _____ the sofa _____ the living room.
8 극장 앞에서 5시 반에 만나자.	Let's meet _____ _____ _____ the theater _____ 5:30.
9 7월에는 종종 비가 온다.	It often rains _____ _____.
10 천장에 모기 두 마리가 있다.	There are two mosquitoes _____ _____ _____.
11 그녀는 보통 금요일마다 장을 보러 간다.	She usually goes grocery shopping _____ _____.
12 그 상점은 일요일 아침에는 10시에 문을 연다.	The shop opens _____ 10 o'clock _____ _____ _____.
13 토끼 한 마리가 덤불 뒤에 숨어 있다.	A rabbit _____ _____ _____ the bush.
14 그 배는 다리 밑을 지나가고 있다.	The ship _____ _____ _____ the bridge.
15 달은 지구와 태양 사이에 있다.	The moon _____ _____ the earth _____ the sun.

STEP 2 배운 문장을 다시 한번 쓰면서 외워보세요. Score _____ / 15

	Korean	English
1	우리는 정오에 점심을 먹는다.	We have
2	그 공연은 8월 24일에 있다.	The concert
3	그는 2010년에 서울로 이사 갔다.	
4	그녀는 버스 정류장에 서있다.	
5	한 남자가 내 옆에 앉았다.	
6	밤에 혼자 걷는 것은 위험하다.	It is
7	나는 거실 소파 위에서 너의 노트북을 봤어.	
8	극장 앞에서 5시 반에 만나자.	Let's
9	7월에는 종종 비가 온다.	It
10	천장에 모기 두 마리가 있다.	There are
11	그녀는 보통 금요일마다 장을 보러 간다.	She usually goes
12	그 상점은 일요일 아침에는 10시에 문을 연다.	The shop
13	토끼 한 마리가 덤불 뒤에 숨어 있다.	
14	그 배는 다리 밑을 지나가고 있다.	The ship
15	달은 지구와 태양 사이에 있다.	The moon

접속사

STEP I 배운 문장을 쓰면서 외워보세요.

Score _____ / 15

	Korean	English
1	내가 런던에 도착할 때, 너에게 문자 할게.	_____ _____ _____ in London, I'll _____ _____.
2	그는 대학을 마친 후 직장을 구했다.	He got a job _____ _____ _____ college.
3	나는 크리스마스 날에 눈이 오길 바란다.	_____ _____ _____ it snows on Christmas day.
4	나는 그가 복권에 당첨되었다는 것을 믿을 수 없다.	_____ _____ _____ _____ he won the lottery.
5	나가기 전에 창문 좀 닫아줄래?	Can you close the window _____ _____ _____ _____ ?
6	잠이 든 후에, 그는 이상한 꿈을 꿨다.	_____ _____ _____ _____, he had a strange dream.
7	그 소식을 들었을 때, 그녀는 기뻐서 뛰었다.	_____ _____ _____ the news, she jumped with joy.
8	나는 그가 유머 감각이 뛰어나다고 생각해.	_____ _____ _____ he has a good sense of humor.
9	우리는 흡연이 우리 건강에 나쁘다는 것을 안다.	_____ _____ _____ _____ _____ bad for our health.
10	사람들은 네 잎 클로버가 그들에게 행운을 가져다 준다고 믿는다.	_____ _____ _____ a four-leaf clover _____ _____ good luck.
11	Jack은 버스를 놓쳐서 학교에 늦었다.	Jack was late for school _____ _____ _____ the bus.
12	나는 감기에 걸렸을 때 뜨거운 차를 마신다.	I drink hot tea _____ _____ have _____ _____.
13	너는 화성에 생명체가 있다고 생각하니?	_____ _____ _____ _____ there is life on Mars?
14	나는 우리가 그것을 해냈다는 것을 믿을 수 없다.	_____ _____ _____ _____ we made it.
15	나는 네가 1등 상을 받은 지 몰랐어.	_____ _____ _____ _____ you won the first prize.

STEP 2 배운 문장을 다시 한번 쓰면서 외워보세요. Score _____ / 15

	Korean	English
1	내가 런던에 도착할 때, 너에게 문자 할게.	When
2	그는 대학을 마친 후 직장을 구했다.	He
3	나는 크리스마스 날에 눈이 오길 바란다.	I hope
4	나는 그가 복권에 당첨되었다는 것을 믿을 수 없다.	
5	나가기 전에 창문 좀 닫아줄래?	Can you
6	잠이 든 후에, 그는 이상한 꿈을 꿨다.	After
7	그 소식을 들었을 때, 그녀는 기뻐서 뛰었다.	When
8	나는 그가 유머 감각이 뛰어나다고 생각해.	
9	우리는 흡연이 우리 건강에 나쁘다는 것을 안다.	
10	사람들은 네 잎 클로버가 그들에게 행운을 가져다 준다고 믿는다.	People
11	Jack은 버스를 놓쳐서 학교에 늦었다.	Jack
12	나는 감기에 걸렸을 때 뜨거운 차를 마신다.	I
13	너는 화성에 생명체가 있다고 생각하니?	Do you
14	나는 우리가 그것을 해냈다는 것을 믿을 수 없다.	
15	나는 네가 1등 상을 받은 지 몰랐어.	I

STEP I   배운 문장을 쓰면서 외워보세요.   Score _____ / 15

Korean	English
1 다른 사람들에게 친절해라.	_____ _____ to _____ _____.
2 소금 좀 건네주세요.	Please _____ _____ _____ _____.
3 네 남동생과 싸우지 마라.	_____ _____ with your brother.
4 복도에서 뛰지 마라.	_____ _____ in the hallway.
5 그 우유를 냉장고에 넣어라.	_____ _____ _____ in the refrigerator.
6 줄을 서세요.	_____ _____ line, please.
7 음악 소리 좀 낮춰주세요.	Please _____ _____ the music.
8 밤에는 시끄럽게 하지 마라.	_____ _____ _____ at night.
9 다시는 늦지 마라.	_____ _____ _____ again.
10 네 카메라 가져오는 거 잊지 마.	_____ _____ _____ _____ your camera.
11 모퉁이에서 우회전해라.	_____ _____ at the corner.
12 그것들을 안전한 곳에 보관해라.	_____ _____ in a _____ _____.
13 이 약을 하루 세 번 복용해라.	_____ this medicine _____ _____ _____ _____.
14 쓰레기를 쓰레기통에 넣어라.	_____ the trash _____ the trash can.
15 네 선생님에게 무례하게 하지 마라.	_____ _____ _____ to your teacher.

STEP 2 배운 문장을 다시 한번 쓰면서 외워보세요. Score _____ / 15

	Korean	English
1	다른 사람들에게 친절해라.	
2	소금 좀 건네주세요.	Please
3	네 남동생과 싸우지 마라.	
4	복도에서 뛰지 마라.	
5	그 우유를 냉장고에 넣어라.	
6	줄을 서세요.	Stand
7	음악 소리 좀 낮춰주세요.	Please
8	밤에는 시끄럽게 하지 마라.	
9	다시는 늦지 마라.	
10	네 카메라 가져오는 거 잊지 마.	
11	모퉁이에서 우회전해라.	
12	그것들을 안전한 곳에 보관해라.	Keep
13	이 약을 하루 세 번 복용해라.	
14	쓰레기를 쓰레기통에 넣어라.	
15	네 선생님에게 무례하게 하지 마라.	

STEP I 배운 문장을 쓰면서 외워보세요.

Score _____ / 15

Korean	English
1 그것은 정말 흥미로운 책이구나!	_____ _____ _____ _____ it is!
2 그는 정말 훌륭한 일을 했구나!	_____ _____ _____ _____ he did!
3 그 수박은 정말 크구나!	_____ _____ the watermelon _____!
4 정말 춥구나!	_____ _____ it is!
5 너는 정말 용감하구나!	_____ _____ you _____!
6 그녀는 정말 행복해 보이는구나!	_____ _____ she _____!
7 그들은 정말 좋은 이웃들이구나!	_____ _____ _____ they are!
8 그녀는 정말 사랑스러운 미소를 가지고 있구나!	_____ _____ _____ _____ she has!
9 너는 정말 멋진 셔츠를 입고 있구나!	_____ _____ _____ you are wearing!
10 정말 긴 하루였어!	_____ _____ _____ it _____!
11 정말 피곤하구나!	_____ _____ I _____!
12 그녀는 정말 아름답게 춤추는구나!	_____ _____ she _____!
13 그것은 정말 흥미진진한 경기였어!	_____ _____ _____ it _____!
14 그는 정말 빨리 달리고 있구나!	_____ _____ he _____ _____!
15 너는 정말 멋진 사진들을 찍었구나!	_____ _____ pictures you _____!

STEP 2   배운 문장을 다시 한번 쓰면서 외워보세요.   Score _____ / 15

	Korean	English
1	그것은 정말 흥미로운 책이구나!	What
2	그는 정말 훌륭한 일을 했구나!	What
3	그 수박은 정말 크구나!	How
4	정말 춥구나!	How
5	너는 정말 용감하구나!	How
6	그녀는 정말 행복해 보이는구나!	How
7	그들은 정말 좋은 이웃들이구나!	What
8	그녀는 정말 사랑스러운 미소를 가지고 있구나!	What
9	너는 정말 멋진 셔츠를 입고 있구나!	What
10	정말 긴 하루였어!	What
11	정말 피곤하구나!	How
12	그녀는 정말 아름답게 춤추는구나!	How
13	그것은 정말 흥미진진한 경기였어!	What
14	그는 정말 빨리 달리고 있구나!	How
15	너는 정말 멋진 사진들을 찍었구나!	What

STEP I 배운 문장을 쓰면서 외워보세요.

Score _____ / 15

Korean	English
1 그 정원은 아름다워, 그렇지 않니?	The garden is beautiful, _____ _____?
2 넌 내 가장 친한 친구야, 그렇지 않니?	You are my best friend, _____ _____?
3 그 영화는 지루했어, 그렇지 않니?	The movie was boring, _____ _____?
4 그녀는 영어를 할 수 있어, 그렇지 않니?	She can speak English, _____ _____?
5 그들은 내일 떠날 거야, 그렇지 않니?	They will leave tomorrow, _____ _____?
6 나는 그 차를 사지 말아야 해, 그렇지?	I shouldn't buy the car, _____ _____?
7 그들은 서로를 몰라, 그렇지?	They _____ _____ each other, _____ _____?
8 너는 그를 저녁식사에 초대할 거지, 그렇지 않니?	You will _____ _____ to dinner, _____ _____?
9 너는 매운 음식을 좋아하지 않아, 그렇지?	You _____ _____ spicy food, _____ _____?
10 그 슈퍼마켓은 자정에 문을 닫아, 그렇지 않니?	The supermarket _____ at midnight, _____ _____?
11 그들은 어젯밤에 극장에 갔어, 그렇지 않니?	_____ _____ to the theater last night, _____?
12 이 셔츠는 나에게 너무 커, 그렇지 않니?	This shirt _____ _____ _____ for me, _____ _____?
13 너는 대도시에 살아, 그렇지 않니?	_____ _____ in a big city, _____ _____?
14 그 안경은 네 것이야, 그렇지 않니?	The glasses _____ yours, _____ _____?
15 Jack, 네가 내 책을 빌려갔어, 그렇지 않니?	Jack, you _____ my book, _____ _____?

STEP 2 배운 문장을 다시 한번 쓰면서 외워보세요.

Score _____ / 15

Korean	English
1 그 정원은 아름다워, 그렇지 않니?	
2 넌 내 가장 친한 친구야, 그렇지 않니?	
3 그 영화는 지루했어, 그렇지 않니?	The movie
4 그녀는 영어를 할 수 있어, 그렇지 않니?	She can
5 그들은 내일 떠날 거야, 그렇지 않니?	They will
6 나는 그 차를 사지 말아야 해, 그렇지?	I shouldn't
7 그들은 서로를 몰라, 그렇지?	
8 너는 그를 저녁식사에 초대할 거지, 그렇지 않니?	You will
9 너는 매운 음식을 좋아하지 않아, 그렇지?	
10 그 슈퍼마켓은 자정에 문을 닫아, 그렇지 않니?	
11 그들은 어젯밤에 극장에 갔어, 그렇지 않니?	
12 이 셔츠는 나에게 너무 커, 그렇지 않니?	
13 너는 대도시에 살아, 그렇지 않니?	
14 그 안경은 네 것이야, 그렇지 않니?	The glasses
15 Jack, 네가 내 책을 빌려갔어, 그렇지 않니?	Jack,

중학 영작 + 서술형 대비

내공

✳ 전지원, 박혜영

중학 영작문 ①

정 답

DARAKWON

중학 영작 + 서술형 대비

내공

중학
영작문 ①

정 답

다락원

UNIT 01

p.013

LESSON 01 be동사와 인칭대명사

CHECK UP
p.010

1. am
2. is
3. are
4. is
5. are
6. I
7. He
8. They
9. It

SENTENCE PRACTICE 1
p.011

WRITING POINT ❶

1. I am strong.
2. You are a good singer.
3. He is my cousin.
4. She is a middle school student.
5. It is in my bag.
6. The puppy is cute.
7. This notebook is mine.
8. Mr. James is in the classroom.

WRITING POINT ❷

1. You are my friends.
2. You are good neighbors.
3. They are sisters.
4. They are soccer players.
5. We are at the airport.
6. Those games are fun.
7. Philip and Sue are good at math.
8. Tom and I are in the same class.

SENTENCE PRACTICE 2
p.012

1. I am tired and sleepy.
2. Thank you. You are so kind.
3. Her name is Jessica.
4. The man is from Australia.
5. My birthday is in April.
6. They are busy with their work.
7. Rick and I are close friends.
8. You are still young and beautiful.
9. The children are in the swimming pool.
10. These pants are too big for me.

TRY WRITING
p.013

1. The actor is tall and handsome.
2. China is a big country.
3. You are very patient and generous.
4. She is polite to people.
5. My favorite season is summer
6. Jane and I are fifteen years old.
7. My brother is good at sports.
8. The café is on the second floor.
9. The dogs are in the yard.
10. They are on vacation in Hawaii.
11. Mr. Endly is my new English teacher.
12. Her nickname is Dancing Queen.

LESSON 02 be동사의 부정문, 의문문

CHECK UP
p.014

1. am not
2. Are
3. are not
4. Is
5. are not
6. I'm not
7. It isn't / It's not
8. He isn't / He's not
10. They aren't / They're not

SENTENCE PRACTICE 1
p.015

WRITING POINT ❶

1. I am not a good cook.
2. You are not lazy.
3. He is not my brother.
4. She is not in her room.
5. We are not ready yet.
6. This soup is not warm.
7. Those shoes are not mine.

WRITING POINT ❷

1. Are you busy today?
2. Is he free today?
3. Am I your best friend?
4. Is it on the first floor?
5. Are they in the living room?
6. Is Helen a lawyer?
7. Are Alex and you the same age?
8. Is the book interesting?

SENTENCE PRACTICE 2

1. I am not a liar.
2. The weather is not cold today.
3. Don't worry. You are not alone.
4. Your notebooks are not on the desk.
5. The shop is not open on Sunday.
6. Are you interested in music?
7. Are your parents strict?
8. Is Minho angry with me?
9. Are we ready to go?
10. Is John still in bed?

TRY WRITING

1. These vegetables are not[aren't] fresh.
2. Is this your bag?
3. Are you free this Saturday?
4. It is not[isn't] my cell phone.
5. Is the movie interesting?
6. We are not[aren't] in class right now.
7. Are Mina and Minji twins?
8. Mr. Brown is not[isn't] married.
9. Pam and Rachel are not[aren't] in the same class.
10. Is blue your favorite color?
11. I am not[I'm not] interested in sports
12. Are you afraid of dogs?

미리 보는 서술형 SCHOOL TEST

1. (1) am　　　(2) are　　　(3) is
2. He is kind and funny.
3. (1) The answer is not[isn't] correct.
   (2) Are they in the living room?
4. (1) They are not[aren't] tall.
   (2) Is he your math teacher?
5. Are you good at
6. (1) is　　　(2) is from　　　(3) is fifteen
   (4) is bulgogi
7. ② is → are　　　⑤ am → are

UNIT 02

LESSON 03 일반동사의 긍정문

CHECK UP

1. play
2. gets
3. buy
4. cries
5. does
6. snows
7. go
8. has
9. freezes

SENTENCE PRACTICE 1

WRITING POINT ❶

1. I eat breakfast every day.
2. You have a nice car.
3. We usually walk to school.
4. They watch TV in the evening.
5. The students wear school uniforms.
6. His parents live in Canada.
7. The girls play tennis very well.
8. Tom and Sally like ice cream.
9. The scientists make robots.

WRITING POINT ❷

1. He lives in that house.
2. He goes to school by bus.
3. She studies medicine.
4. She teaches English at school.
5. Mike enjoys Thai food.
6. My sister has curly hair.
7. The movie starts at 10.
8. The horse runs very fast.
9. Ann buys a cake every Christmas.

SENTENCE PRACTICE 2

1. I go to Jeju Island every summer.
2. We enjoy outdoor sports on weekends.
3. You understand me well all the time.
4. Greg and Kelly study in the library after school.
5. Many foreigners learn Korean these days.
6. He usually eats sandwiches for lunch.
7. The actor speaks three languages.
8. Minsu reads comic books in his free time.
9. She has a nice house with a pool.

10. His dog always barks at me.

p.023

TRY WRITING

1. I get up late in the morning.
2. Jiho plays computer games after dinner.
3. Cathy washes her hair every morning.
4. My grandmother grows tomatoes in her garden.
5. Spiders have eight legs.
6. He walks his dog every day.
7. Mr. and Mrs. Jones have three children.
8. We clean the house every day.
9. Many people ride bicycles in the park.
10. My brother collects coins from other countries.
11. The birds fly very high.
12. This computer needs fixing.

LESSON 04 일반동사의 부정문, 의문문

CHECK UP
p.024

1. don't	2. Do	3. doesn't
4. Do	5. don't	6. doesn't
7. don't	8. Do	9. doesn't
10. Do		

SENTENCE PRACTICE 1
p.025

WRITING POINT ❶

1. I don't eat breakfast.
2. You don't like vegetables.
3. He doesn't drive a car.
4. She doesn't wear glasses.
5. We don't have classes today.
6. They don't live on this street.
7. Kelly doesn't buy many clothes.
8. The bus doesn't stop here.

WRITING POINT ❷

1. Do you know his name?
2. Does he play the drums?
3. Does she speak French?
4. Do we need more time?
5. Do they work on Saturday?

6. Does Nora have a sister?
7. Do Andrew and Mary like dogs?
8. Does your father often cook?

SENTENCE PRACTICE 2
p.026

1. I don't know much about him.
2. It doesn't snow in Australia.
3. We don't have much time.
4. The restaurant doesn't serve breakfast.
5. Judy and Frank don't speak Korean well.
6. Do you play a musical instrument?
7. Does he go to the gym every day?
8. Does your father wear a suit to work?
9. Do Tara and Dave travel a lot?
10. Does the summer vacation start in July?

TRY WRITING
p.027

1. He does not[doesn't] tell lies.
2. I do not[don't] like hot weather.
3. Do you take a walk after dinner?
4. The computer does not[doesn't] work well.
5. Do you make your bed every morning?
6. Does this bus go to the airport?
7. The children do not[don't] feel happy.
8. They do not[don't] sell used things.
9. Does Mr. Lee teach science?
10. John does not[doesn't] have many friends at school.
11. Does it rain a lot in June?
12. Do people in your country use chopsticks?

미리 보는 서술형 SCHOOL TEST
p.028

1. I go to the library.
2. Do they live / they don't / They live
3. (1) We don't have a math test today.
   (2) Do we have a math test today?
4. (1) gets   (2) has   (3) leaves
   (4) arrives
5. doesn't have

6. (1) takes a piano lesson
   (2) goes to the gym
   (3) does her homework
7. ① Do → Does ④ work → works

6. The umbrella wasn't in the car.
7. Lucy and I weren't in the same class.
8. Was he a professor at a university?
9. Was the movie good last night?
10. Were John and Peggy at your birthday party?

UNIT 03

LESSON 05 be동사의 과거형

CHECK UP
p.030

1. was
2. were not
3. Were
4. was not
5. was
6. Were
7. were not
8. Was
9. were

SENTENCE PRACTICE 1
p.031

WRITING POINT ①

1. I was busy yesterday.
2. My mother was a nurse.
3. Sam and I were in the same class.
4. We were late for school this morning.
5. They were at church last Sunday.

WRITING POINT ②

1. He wasn't in London in 2010.
2. They weren't tired.
3. The exam wasn't difficult.
4. The children weren't quiet.

WRITING POINT ③

1. Was he your friend?
2. Were you at home last weekend?
3. Was the hotel comfortable?
4. Were the boys in the park?

SENTENCE PRACTICE 2
p.032

1. It was cold and windy yesterday.
2. My sister was born in May.
3. We were in Sydney last summer.
4. Frankfurt was the capital of Germany.
5. They weren't close to each other.

TRY WRITING
p.033

1. The book was under my bed.
2. David Beckham was my favorite soccer player.
3. Picasso and Van Gogh were great artists.
4. It was my mistake.
5. Were you good at math in high school?
6. Luckily, we weren't[were not] late for school.
7. I was tired after the exam.
8. The party was not[wasn't] fun. It was boring.
9. My parents and I were on vacation last week.
10. Was he in New York in 2016?
11. Were they at the theater last night?
12. He was not[wasn't] a famous singer at the time.

LESSON 06 일반동사의 과거형

CHECK UP
p.034

1. learned
2. wanted
3. passed
4. loved
5. cried
6. enjoyed
7. stopped
8. planned
9. went
10. ate
11. read
12. saw
13. heard
14. knew
15. wrote
16. bought

SENTENCE PRACTICE 1
p.035

WRITING POINT ①

1. We went home early.
2. He passed the exam.
3. It rained all day.
4. Kevin broke the vase.
5. I lost my umbrella.

1. I didn't call you.

2. He didn't buy the shirt.

3. She didn't eat the food.

4. We didn't hear the news.

5. They didn't close the window.

1. Did he drive to work?

2. Did you find your key?

3. Did he fix the computer?

4. Did she finish her homework?

5. Did they win the game?

SENTENCE PRACTICE 2   p.036

1. We went to the movies last Friday.

2. Mr. Brown invited us to dinner.

3. She had a hamburger for lunch.

4. I left my bag on the bus.

5. He didn't wash his hands before eating.

6. They didn't come to my birthday party.

7. The steak didn't taste good.

8. Did he live in England?

9. Did she turn on the air conditioner?

10. Did you brush your teeth after the meal?

TRY WRITING   p.037

1. Chris bought a new guitar.

2. We went shopping last weekend.

3. Did I make a mistake?

4. Rick forgot his homework yesterday.

5. Did they enjoy their holiday?

6. Brad and Angela got married in 2014.

7. Did you skip breakfast this morning?

8. The train did not[didn't] arrive on time.

9. Lucy did not[didn't] meet her friends last week.

10. Lisa cut her finger in art class.

11. Steve did not[didn't] sleep well last night.

12. My brother won the first prize in the writing contest.

LESSON 07 현재진행형

CHECK UP   p.038

1. eat   2. are waiting   3. goes

4. is making   5. visit   6. are sitting

7. is snowing   8. lays   9. are coming

10. drink

SENTENCE PRACTICE 1   p.039

WRITING POINT ❶

1. They are walking along the beach.

2. The girl is sitting on the bench.

3. The boys are riding bicycles.

4. My cat is sleeping on the sofa.

5. It is raining outside.

WRITING POINT ❷

1. She isn't driving a car.

2. You aren't wearing glasses.

3. Julie isn't cooking now.

4. The train isn't running now.

5. They aren't talking on the phone.

WRITING POINT ❸

1. Is he watching TV?

2. Is she reading a book?

3. Are you having a good time?

4. Are they playing volleyball?

5. Are Kevin and Lisa doing their homework?

SENTENCE PRACTICE 2   p.040

1. I am feeding my cat.

2. The children are crossing the street.

3. Robin is lying in bed now.

4. The guests are taking off their coats.

5. Sarah isn't wearing earrings.

6. You aren't telling me the truth.

7. The escalator isn't working at the moment.

8. Are you studying in the library?

9. Are they talking on the phone now?

10. Is Jane practicing the violin in her room?

1. She is drinking a cup of tea.
2. You are singing too loudly.
3. Is he using the copy machine?
4. I am not[I'm not] feeling well today.
5. My father is not[isn't] working at a bank now.
6. Helen is cooking a traditional Korean food.
7. Are you looking for your car keys?
8. A strange man is staring at me.
9. Woojin is taking a hot bath right now.
10. Are you charging your cell phone?
11. My grandmother is watering the flowers in the garden.
12. Are Tom and Rachael waiting for the school bus?

미리 보는 서술형 SCHOOL TEST
p. 042

1. (1) was   (2) Were   (3) weren't
2. He is taking a taekwondo lesson.
3. (1) My dad is making dinner for us.
   (2) My dad made dinner for us.
4. (1) He did not[didn't] pass the exam.
   (2) Did you read the novel?
5. is playing the piano and singing a song
6. I bought / apples / milk
7. (1) woke up   (2) took   (3) met
   (4) ate   (5) was   (6) went

UNIT 04

LESSON 08 will, be going to

CHECK UP
p. 044

1. see   2. be   3. to play
4. drive   5. to meet   6. to fly
7. open   8. to have   9. do
10. to be

WRITING POINT ①

1. I will be at home this evening.
2. I will not be at home this evening.
3. He will have/eat lunch at noon.
4. He will not have/eat lunch at noon.
5. They will come to my party.
6. Will they come to my party?
7. Susan will like this present.
8. Will Susan like this present?

WRITING POINT ②

1. We are going to do it.
2. We aren't going to do it.
3. I am going to watch the movie.
4. I am not going to watch the movie.
5. They are going to visit the museum.
6. Are they going to visit the museum?
7. Mike is going to come to the meeting.
8. Is Mike going to come to the meeting?

SENTENCE PRACTICE 2
p. 046

1. We will wait and see.
2. Eric will drive us to the station.
3. I will not take a bus. I will walk.
4. Some people will not believe this.
5. Will you be at home this evening?
6. I am going to move into a new house next month.
7. He is going to leave for Busan tomorrow.
8. We aren't going to take a test today.
9. Are they going to work this Saturday?
10. My parents aren't going to go out this evening.

TRY WRITING ✏️
p. 047

1. I will[I'll] do my best.
2. We are going to sell this old furniture.
3. They are going to get married next month.
4. Will you be a movie director in the future?
5. His son will be fifteen years old next month.
6. You will not[won't] have any problems.
7. Are you going to wear that dress to the party?

8. They are not[aren't] going to leave tomorrow.

9. Ted is going to fly to London in July.

10. I will[I'll] be ready in five minutes.

11. We are going to have/eat dinner at a nice restaurant.

12. In the future, people will travel to other planets.

LESSON 09 can, may

CHECK UP p.048

1. 능력
2. 허락
3. 능력
4. 추측
5. 능력
6. 허락
7. 허락
8. 추측
9. 능력
10. 허락

SENTENCE PRACTICE 1 p.049

WRITING POINT ❶

1. I can sing the song.
2. I cannot sing the song.
3. He can answer the phone right now.
4. He cannot answer the phone right now.
5. We can use the library.
6. Can we use the library?
7. Judy can ride a bicycle.
8. Can Judy ride a bicycle?

WRITING POINT ❷

1. I may pass the exam.
2. I may not pass the exam.
3. He may be sick today.
4. He may not be sick today.
5. You may use my car tomorrow.
6. You may not use my car tomorrow.
7. May I sit here?
8. May I ask a question?

SENTENCE PRACTICE 2 p.050

1. She can speak English well.
2. We cannot[can't] live without water.
3. You cannot[can't] do this to me.
4. Can you help me with my homework?

---

5. Tom can swim and play table tennis very well.
6. May I help you?
7. It may snow next week.
8. She may not like seafood.
9. You may go out with your friends.
10. May I see your passport?

TRY WRITING p.051

1. Can Dave fix this car?
2. Can you speak a little louder?
3. You may/can use the computers in the library.
4. I may go to the movies tonight.
5. May/Can I try on these shoes? / May/Can I try these shoes on?
6. Some people can speak three languages.
7. My grandfather cannot[can't] read without glasses.
8. I cannot[can't] find my key anywhere.
9. He can run 100 meters in 12. seconds.
10. Your purse may be on the table.
11. You may not/cannot[can't] park your car here.
12. You may not/cannot[can't] take photos in this museum.

LESSON 10 must, have to, should

CHECK UP p.052

1. 조언
2. 금지
3. 의무/필요
4. 조언
5. 의무
6. 조언
7. 불필요
8. 의무
9. 불필요

SENTENCE PRACTICE 1 p.053

WRITING POINT ❶

1. You must tell the truth.
2. You must not tell the truth.
3. He must go there.
4. He must not go there.

1. We <u>have to wait</u> for him.
2. We <u>don't have to wait</u> for him.
3. She <u>has to take</u> a taxi.
4. She <u>doesn't have to take</u> a taxi.

WRITING POINT ③

1. You <u>should watch</u> the movie.
2. You <u>should not watch</u> the movie.
3. They <u>should work</u> late.
4. They <u>should not work</u> late.

SENTENCE PRACTICE 2
p.054

1. You <u>must answer</u> all the questions.
2. Students <u>must hand in</u> their homework by tomorrow.
3. Jane <u>must not eat</u> too much junk food.
4. He <u>has to get up</u> early tomorrow morning.
5. I <u>have to be home</u> by 7 o'clock.
6. You <u>don't have to say</u> sorry.
7. Sally <u>doesn't have to lose weight</u>.
8. You <u>should exercise regularly</u>.
9. He <u>should not stay up too late</u>.
10. Jake <u>should spend more time</u> with his family.

TRY WRITING
p.055

1. You must keep your promise.
2. We should drink enough water every day.
3. I have to finish my homework today.
4. People must not[mustn't] smoke in public places.
5. You should drive carefully at night.
6. You don't have to worry about it.
7. They should not[shouldn't] buy the house.
8. You must not[mustn't] use your cell phone during the class.
9. You should brush your teeth three times a day.
10. John has to learn English for his job.
11. Joe and Lucy must catch the train.
12. They don't have to pay for dinner.

미리 보는 서술형 SCHOOL TEST
p.056

1. is going to
2. (1) Will he come to the party tonight?
   (2) I'm going to meet Susan this Friday.
3. can play the guitar
4. He may not be at home.
5. (1) have to recycle
   (2) don't have to take
6. (1) must take off your shoes
   (2) must not take photos
7. (1) should not[shouldn't] be
   (2) should listen to
   (3) should not[shouldn't] talk

UNIT 05

LESSON 1 when, where

CHECK UP
p.058

1. Where
2. When
3. When
4. Where
5. When
6. When
7. Where
8. Where
9. When
10. Where

SENTENCE PRACTICE 1
p.059

WRITING POINT ①

1. <u>When is</u> Jane's birthday?
2. <u>When is</u> the soccer game?
3. <u>Where are</u> you from?
4. <u>Where is</u> your school bag?
5. <u>When were</u> you born?
6. <u>Where was</u> he last night?
7. <u>When are</u> they going to leave?
8. <u>Where is</u> she going?

WRITING POINT ②

1. <u>When do</u> you go to bed?
2. <u>When does</u> he practice tennis?
3. <u>Where do</u> you buy your clothes?
4. <u>Where does</u> she go on Sundays?

5. When did you meet her?

6. When did she call you?

7. Where did you find your bag?

8. Where did he leave his umbrella?

p. 060

SENTENCE PRACTICE 2

1. Where is Jack at the moment?

2. When is Mother's Day in America?

3. Where is your English teacher from?

4. Where were you after school?

5. When are you going to do your homework?

6. Where do you usually go shopping?

7. When does the movie start?

8. When does the next bus arrive?

9. Where did you visit in Europe?

10. When did you lose your sunglasses?

TRY WRITING

p. 061

1. Where is his hometown?

2. Where are your parents?

3. When is your housewarming party?

4. Where do koalas live?

5. When does the department store open?

6. Where is the nearest bus stop?

7. When did you travel to Japan?

8. When did the accident happen?

9. Where was the missing child?

10. Where did you buy the dress?

11. When did she lose her tablet PC?

12. When does the rainy season start in Thailand?

LESSON 12 who, what

CHECK UP

p. 062

1. What	2. Who	3. Who
4. What	5. What	6. Who
7. What	8. Who	

SENTENCE PRACTICE 1

p. 063

WRITING POINT ❶

1. Who is that girl?

2. Who are your best friends?

3. What is your address?

4. What was your first job?

5. What color is his car?

WRITING POINT ❷

1. Who do you work with?

2. What does she do on the weekend?

3. Who did they go with?

4. What did you buy at the mall?

WRITING POINT ❸

1. Who is watching TV?

2. What is in the box?

3. Who cleaned the room?

4. What happened to him?

SENTENCE PRACTICE 2

p. 064

1. Who are the people in the picture?

2. What is the matter with you?

3. What was your major in college?

4. Who do you like the most?

5. Who did he invite to the party?

6. What does this word mean?

7. What time do you usually go to bed?

8. Who is sitting on the sofa?

9. Who stole his wallet yesterday?

10. What fell off the table?

TRY WRITING

p. 065

1. Who is your twin sister?

2. Who is in the kitchen?

3. Who made these sandwiches?

4. What was your biggest mistake?

5. Who turned off the alarm?

6. What do you usually do in your free time?

7. Who do you respect the most?

8. What time does your school start?

9. What do you want for your birthday?

10. Who is using the computer?

11. What is so special about your girlfriend?

12. What looked interesting in the picture?

CHECK UP p.066

1. Why 2. How 3. Why
4. Why 5. How 6. Why
7. How 8. Why 9. How
10. How

SENTENCE PRACTICE 1
p.067

WRITING POINT ①

1. Why is she so happy?
2. Why are the children laughing?
3. How are you today?
4. Why were you late for class?
5. How was your Christmas?

WRITING POINT ②

1. Why does he like Korea?
2. Why did you call me?
3. How do they travel?
4. How did they meet each other?

WRITING POINT ③

1. How old is your brother?
2. How far is the subway station?
3. How often do you wash your hair?
4. How many questions did he ask?

SENTENCE PRACTICE 2
p.068

1. How is the weather in London?
2. Why was he late for the meeting?
3. How was your trip to Spain?
4. How does this machine work?
5. Why does he always complain?
6. How do you know his name?
7. How old is his son?
8. How often do you visit your grandparents?
9. How many times do you eat out a month?
10. How far is your school from here?

TRY WRITING
p.069

1. How is the weather in your country?
2. How was your math test?
3. Why do you like summer?

4. Why was your father upset yesterday?
5. How do you spell your name?
6. How did you get to work this morning?
7. Why are you in a hurry?
8. Why is she crying?
9. How many tickets do you need?
10. How often do you brush your teeth?
11. Why did he quit his job?
12. How many times did you ask her out?

미리 보는 서술형 SCHOOL TEST
p.070

1. (1) Who (2) Where (3) How often
2. (1) What is your name?
   (2) When is your birthday?
   (3) Where are you from?
3. (1) When did he meet his friends?
   (2) What time do you usually get up?
4. How many brothers and sisters do you have?
5. What did you do
6. (1) Who is your favorite teacher?
   (2) What subject does he teach?
7. (1) What is the title
   (2) Where does / take place

UNIT 06

CHECK UP p.072

1. There 2. It 3. There
4. It 5. There 6. there
7. It 8. There

SENTENCE PRACTICE 1
p.073

WRITING POINT ①

1. There is a window in this room.
2. There isn't a window in this room.

3. There are many cars on the road.

4. There aren't many cars on the road.

5. There is a bank near here.

6. Is there a bank near here?

7. There are children in the park.

8. Are there children in the park?

WRITING POINT ②

1. It is raining outside.

2. It isn't cold today.

3. It is nearly seven o'clock.

4. It is August 1st.

5. It is my birthday today.

6. It isn't far from here.

7. It is very dark in here.

8. What time is it now?

9. What day is it today?

SENTENCE PRACTICE 2   p.074

1. There is a big tree in the garden.

2. There are thirty students in our class.

3. There isn't any water in the glass.

4. Is there a parking lot near here?

5. How many people are there in your family?

6. It rains a lot in summer.

7. It is very hot in here.

8. What date is it today?

9. It was Teacher's Day yesterday.

10. It is 10 kilometers to the airport from here.

TRY WRITING   p.075

1. There is a house on the top of the hill.

2. Is it raining outside?

3. It was warm and sunny yesterday.

4. There are four seasons in a year.

5. Is there any mail for me?

6. It is only 10 o'clock.

7. It is Christmas today!

8. Are there any good restaurants near here?

9. There aren't many flowers in the garden.

10. It is November 15th.

11. There is a concert in the park this evening.

12. It takes 10 minutes by bike.

LESSON 15 감각동사+형용사

CHECK UP   p.076

1. feels   2. looks like   3. sounds

4. look   5. felt   6. feel like

7. looks like   8. tastes   9. smells like

10. looks

SENTENCE PRACTICE 1   p.077

WRITING POINT ①

1. They all look different.

2. This blanket feels warm.

3. Her voice sounds beautiful.

4. This fruit tea tastes sweet.

5. The cookies smell delicious.

6. His dog looks very smart.

7. The vegetables don't look fresh.

8. The piano doesn't sound good.

9. Does it taste good?

WRITING POINT ②

1. This picture looks like a photo.

2. This blouse feels like silk.

3. It sounds like a good plan.

4. It smells like Indian food.

5. This meat tastes like chicken.

6. Mina looks like her mother.

7. They don't look like each other.

8. That doesn't sound like a good idea.

9. What does he look like?

SENTENCE PRACTICE 2   p.078

1. You look lovely in that dress.

2. This medicine tastes bitter.

3. This sofa feels comfortable.

4. The flute sounds beautiful.

5. This room smells weird.

6. He looks like a good teacher.

7. This shampoo smells like roses.

8. It sounds like an interesting topic.

9. This ice cream tastes like green tea.

10. This pillow feels like a stone.

p.079

1. That sounds like a joke.

2. This song sounds familiar.

3. The movie star looks like a Greek statue.

4. His explanation sounds difficult.

5. This handkerchief feels soft.

6. The map of Italy looks like a boot.

7. The people in this picture look happy.

8. This perfume smells nice.

9. I feel lonely without you.

10. I sometimes feel like a genius.

11. Dave felt nervous before the speech.

12. The fruit looks like a strawberry but (it) tastes like a pineapple.

LESSON 16 수여동사

p.080

1. Ryan gave me a box of candy.

2. I will lend you my notebook.

3. Mary made her daughter a pretty doll.

4. Jim told us his plans.

5. He asked me a lot of questions.

6. John showed me his new cell phone.

7. Jessica sent her friend an email.

8. She teaches her kids English.

9. Jane's mother bought her a dress.

10. May I ask you some questions?

SENTENCE PRACTICE 1

p.081

WRITING POINT ❶

1. They sent us a fax.

2. I wrote Mike an email.

3. He showed me a picture.

4. Karen told me a secret.

5. I lent Jane my camera.

6. Mr. Kim teaches us math.

7. I bought my sister a book.

8. He made us pizza.

9. He asked me a question.

WRITING POINT ❷

1. They sent a fax to us.

2. I wrote an email to Mike.

3. He showed a picture to me.

4. Karen told a secret to me.

5. I lent my camera to Jane.

6. Mr. Kim teaches math to us.

7. I bought a book for my sister.

8. He made pizza for us.

9. He asked a question of me.

SENTENCE PRACTICE 2

p.082

1. He lent me his notebook.

2. Did you send Mary the parcel?

3. I wrote my teacher a thank-you letter.

4. Can you bring me a glass of water?

5. You can ask me any questions during the class.

6. I bought a toy car for my brother.

7. I will lend 1,000 won to you if you need.

8. My mom made a huge cake for me.

9. Lucy showed her painting to her classmates.

10. They always tell the truth to each other.

TRY WRITING

p.083

1. Frank told us a funny story. / Frank told a funny story to us.

2. You should not[shouldn't] tell me a lie. / You should not[shouldn't] tell a lie to me.

3. The trip gave me a special experience. / The trip gave a special experience to me.

4. My uncle sent me a present on my birthday. / My uncle sent a present to me on my birthday.

5. My dad cooks us dinner once a week. / My dad cooks dinner for us once a week.

6. Linda made me a nice hat. / Linda made a nice hat for me.

7. Steve doesn't lend anyone his car. / Steve doesn't lend his car to anyone.

8. Mindy taught me some Chinese characters. / Mindy taught some Chinese characters to me.

9. He bought her daughter a puppy. / He bought a puppy for her daughter.

10. The reporters asked the girl a lot of questions. / The reporters asked a lot of questions of the girl.

11. The book taught me a lot of lessons. / The book taught a lot of lessons to me.

12. He gave us the vegetables from his garden. / He gave the vegetables from his garden to us.

미리 보는 서술형 SCHOOL TEST

p.084

1. It is

2. It takes 5 minutes on foot.

3. (1) is a dog   (2) are two books
   (3) is a picture

4. (1) feels   (2) tastes   (3) look

5. (1) His voice sounds friendly.
   (2) It sounds like a good idea.

6. (1) She sent her family her pictures.
   (2) I will make my dad delicious cookies.

7. (1) lent an interesting book to me
   (2) a hairpin for my sister

UNIT 07

LESSON 17 to부정사의 명사적 용법

CHECK UP

p.086

1. 만나는 것을   2. 배우는 것은   3. 오는 것을
4. 되는 것(이다)   5. 사는 것은   6. 돕는 것은
7. 여행하는 것을   8. 공부하는 것(이다)
9. 이기는 것은

SENTENCE PRACTICE 1

p.087

WRITING POINT ①

1. It is difficult to learn Chinese.

2. It is fun to go camping.

3. It is fun to ride a bicycle.

4. It is important to help others.

5. It is important to eat healthy food.

WRITING POINT ②

1. My plan is to save money.

2. My hobby is to read novels.

3. My hobby is to listen to music.

4. My dream is to be/become an artist.

5. My dream is to be/become a cook.

WRITING POINT ③

1. I want to buy the book.

2. They plan to clean the house.

3. They plan to wash the dishes.

4. You need to wear glasses.

5. You need to tell them the truth.

SENTENCE PRACTICE 2

p.088

1. It is impossible to get an A+ on the math exam.

2. It is never boring to live in Seoul.

3. It is healthy to eat vegetables.

4. It is not easy to take care of a baby.

5. My wish is to live in Hawaii with my family.

6. My plan is to get a haircut after class.

7. His dream is to be president.

8. Jim and Sue want to spend time together.

9. Mary likes to take pictures.

10. Why did you decide to be a singer?

TRY WRITING

p.089

1. It is not easy to get up at 6 in the morning.

2. She wants to play the cello.

3. Eric promised to pick me up at the airport.

4. My homework is to write about my special talent.

5. It is a good idea to learn a foreign language.

6. My dream is to become an astronaut.

7. It is good to drink a glass of milk every day.

8. My plan is to do push-ups every day.

9. It is impossible to finish the work by tomorrow.

10. We plan to visit the nursing home this weekend.

11. Somi wants to get a doll for her birthday.

12. It was very easy to solve the math problem.

p.090

1. 먹을
2. 합격하기 위해
3. 읽을
4. 앉을
5. 날리기 위해
6. 일하기 위해
7. 입을
8. 만나기 위해
9. 할
10. 묻기 위해

SENTENCE PRACTICE 1 p.091

WRITING POINT ①

1. He has a lot of work to do.
2. I don't have any money to spend.
3. Do you have time to talk to me?
4. The dog is looking for something to eat.
5. You need a jacket to wear at night.
6. I don't have time to go shopping.
7. He has many friends to help him.
8. There are many places to visit in Korea.
9. I need a pen to write with.

WRITING POINT ②

1. I went to the library to study.
2. We went to the beach to swim.
3. He saved money to buy a new bike.
4. I cleaned the house to help my mom.
5. He is studying to pass the exam.
6. My family went out to have/eat dinner.
7. They looked at the map to find the way.
8. He turned on the radio to listen to music.
9. She went to Paris to see the Eiffel Tower.

SENTENCE PRACTICE 2 p.092

1. Everyone needs someone to love.
2. I have a lot of homework to do this week.
3. We have to find a way to solve this problem.
4. There is nothing to worry about.
5. They are looking for a house to live in.
6. He goes jogging every morning to lose weight.
7. We got up early to see the sunrise.
8. I just called you to say hello.
9. I turned on the computer to write an email.
10. Helen is saving money to travel the world.

TRY WRITING p.093

1. I went to the park to walk my dog.
2. It is time to have lunch.
3. The man has three dogs to take care of.
4. You should wear sunglasses to protect your eyes.
5. He introduced a way to reduce air pollution.
6. Minsu studied all night to get good grades.
7. Do you have a pen to write with?
8. You have the right to say no.
9. They are collecting money to help people in need.
10. To climb Mt. Everest, he left for Nepal.
11. The scientists had a meeting to discuss global warming.
12. Kelly and Paul had nothing to talk about.

LESSON |9 동명사

p.094

1. playing
2. to do
3. writing
4. traveling / to travel
5. to go
6. talking
7. to move
8. smoking
9. learning / to learn
10. to visit

SENTENCE PRACTICE 1 p.095

WRITING POINT ①

1. Dancing is great fun.
2. Being/Staying at home all day is boring.
3. Visiting new places is exciting.
4. Exercising every day is not easy.
5. Drinking enough water is good for you.

WRITING POINT ②

1. My hobby is taking pictures.
2. His job is driving a bus.
3. My goal is learning a new language.
4. My dream is studying abroad.
5. My favorite thing is playing basketball.

WRITING POINT ③

1. I enjoy watching movies.
2. The baby kept crying.
3. She avoids eating late at night.

4. He doesn't mind helping others.

5. They finished doing their homework.

p.096

SENTENCE PRACTICE 2

1. Texting is easy and quick.

2. Giving up easily is a bad habit.

3. Building a house takes a lot of time.

4. His secret to success is always doing his best.

5. My favorite thing is eating ice cream after a meal.

6. My goal is running 5 kilometers every day.

7. I enjoy going hiking in my free time.

8. The mechanic finished fixing my car.

9. He kept complaining about his job.

10. Peter gave up losing weight.

TRY WRITING

p.097

1. Her job is helping sick people.

2. Reading English novels is not easy.

3. I sometimes enjoy being alone.

4. My dream is meeting the movie star one day.

5. They kept talking during the class.

6. Sadly, Jina gave up going to music school.

7. Keeping a diary every day is a good habit.

8. My goal is getting a good score in math.

9. Getting enough sleep is important for your health.

10. I finished reading the Harry Potter series.

11. You should avoid eating too much junk food.

12. Surfing the Internet is sometimes a waste of time.

미리 보는 서술형 SCHOOL TEST

p.098

1. (1) It is dangerous to swim in this river.
   (2) It is impossible to live without water.

2. to be a famous singer

3. (1) to study math
   (2) to play tennis
   (3) to meet his friends

4. no friends to play with

5. (1) to have/eat lunch
   (2) to walk her dog

6. (1) Sleeping   (2) Playing basketball

7. (1) to buy   (2) skiing   (3) to send
   (4) doing

UNIT 08

LESSON 20 수량 형용사, 빈도부사

CHECK UP

p.100

1. many   2. much   3. Many

4. much

5. He is angry with me.

6. I get up late on the weekend.

7. You should watch out for cars.

8. I will make the same mistake.

SENTENCE PRACTICE 1

p.101

WRITING POINT ①

1. Are there many people in the park?

2. Do you have much homework today?

3. I don't have many clothes to wear.

4. We don't have much time.

WRITING POINT ②

1. John has a lot of friends.

2. Sally drinks a lot of tea.

3. They asked a lot of questions.

4. We bought a lot of food.

WRITING POINT ③

1. I usually walk to school.

2. Do you often exercise?

3. His room is always clean.

4. I will never see him again.

5. You can always use my computer.

SENTENCE PRACTICE 2

1. She doesn't eat much meat.
2. I have so many things to tell you.
3. We didn't have much rain last summer.
4. I can't see many stars in the sky tonight.
5. There is a lot of snow on the mountains.
6. We have a lot of problems to solve.
7. Jessica got a lot of cards on her birthday.
8. It is often cloudy in London.
9. My car sometimes breaks down.
10. You should always be honest.

TRY WRITING

1. I usually go to bed before 10 p.m.
2. You should not[shouldn't] eat too many sweets.
3. We do not[don't] have much time to finish the work.
4. Too much love is sometimes bad for children.
5. There are a lot of/lots of books on world history.
6. I met a lot of/lots of foreigners at the festival.
7. There were not[weren't] many guests at the hotel.
8. My father is always busy at work.
9. He never says "thank you."
10. She spends too much money on clothes.
11. You can always ask me for help.
12. You should eat a lot of/lots of vegetables for your health.

LESSON 2 | 비교급, 최상급

 CHECK UP

1. longer / longest
2. better / best
3. cuter / cutest
4. more difficult / most difficult
5. earlier / earliest
6. more / most
7. younger / youngest
8. hotter / hottest
9. more interesting / most interesting
10. more popular / most popular

SENTENCE PRACTICE 1

WRITING POINT ❶

1. Tom is shorter than Mike.
2. India is hotter than England.
3. My bag is heavier than yours.
4. For me, English is easier than math.
5. I get up earlier than my sister.
6. The movie is more boring than the book.
7. This cake is more delicious than that one.
8. Soccer is more exciting than golf.

WRITING POINT ❷

1. January is the coldest month of the year.
2. Nick is the fastest player on the team.
3. David is the best student in the class.
4. Sally is the youngest of the three.
5. The Nile is the longest river in the world.
6. This car is the most expensive in the shop.
7. This question is the most difficult of all.
8. Sharks are the most dangerous animals in the sea.

SENTENCE PRACTICE 2

1. My computer is newer than yours.
2. Mangos are sweeter than oranges.
3. Snow White is more beautiful than the witch.
4. My dad cooks better than my mom.
5. There are more girls than boys in the class.
6. He is the richest man in the world.
7. Today is the happiest day in my life.
8. For me, science is the most difficult subject.
9. This is the cheapest restaurant in the town.
10. It is the quickest way to get to the airport.

TRY WRITING

1. I have longer hair than my sister.
2. My grandmother is the oldest person in my family.
3. Today is warmer than yesterday.
4. Kate is prettier than Diana.

5. He is the fastest runner in the world.

6. Turtles live longer than other animals.

7. The first question is more difficult than the second question.

8. This is the most expensive hotel in the city.

9. What is the highest mountain in the world?

10. Skiing is more dangerous than fishing.

11. Ice hockey is the most popular sport in Canada.

12. What is the most important thing in your life?

LESSON 22 원급 비교

CHECK UP   p.108

1. fast   2. fatter   3. beautiful
4. taller   5. strong   6. hardest
7. difficult   8. safer   9. largest
10. worse

SENTENCE PRACTICE 1   p.109

WRITING POINT ❶

1. This bed is as hard as a rock.

2. Her skin is as white as snow.

3. The water is as cold as ice.

4. Time is as important as money.

5. The blanket is as light as a feather.

6. This pizza is as delicious as the pasta.

7. This problem is as easy as ABC.

8. He eats as much as you.

9. Jane plays tennis as well as Jim.

WRITING POINT ❷

1. My hair is not as long as yours.

2. Silver is not as heavy as gold.

3. The moon is not as bright as the sun.

4. Greece is not as large as France.

5. Volleyball is not as popular as soccer.

6. This summer is not as hot as last summer.

7. His idea is not as good as yours.

8. This painting is not as old as that one.

9. John doesn't work as hard as Mark.

SENTENCE PRACTICE 2   p.110

1. Bill is as tall as his father.

2. The bracelet is as expensive as the necklace.

3. This new sofa is as comfortable as the old one.

4. I can ride a bike as well as you.

5. I try to exercise as often as I can.

6. I am not as tired as you.

7. A lake is not as big as an ocean.

8. Money is not as important as good health.

9. Ostriches cannot run as fast as cheetahs.

10. The bus was not as crowded as usual.

TRY WRITING   p.111

1. My mother is as old as my father.

2. The tree is not[isn't] as tall as the house.

3. This blouse is as smooth as silk.

4. I can jump as high as you.

5. Paul cannot[can't] dance as well as Steve.

6. Mozart was as great as Beethoven.

7. Tom is not[isn't] as clever as Jerry.

8. He is running as fast as he can.

9. This apple is not[isn't] as sweet as that one.

10. The new shoes are not[aren't] as comfortable as the old ones.

11. I do not[don't] watch TV as much as you.

12. The new teacher is as nice as Mr. Kim.

미리 보는 서술형 SCHOOL TEST   p.112

1. (1) many   (2) much   (3) a lot of
2. (1) more books
   (2) easier than
3. (1) more expensive than
   (2) the most expensive
4. (1) My sister is the shortest in my family.
   (2) What is the largest animal in the world?
5. Sora is the tallest of the three.
6. as heavy as
7. run as fast as the car

UNIT 09

LESSON 23 전치사

CHECK UP
p.114

1. in
2. at
3. in
4. on
5. in
6. on
7. under
8. between

SENTENCE PRACTICE 1
p.115

WRITING POINT ①

1. School is over <u>at</u> 3 o'clock.
2. I get up early <u>in</u> the morning.
3. He plays tennis <u>on</u> Saturdays.
4. We have lunch <u>at</u> noon.
5. Her birthday is <u>in</u> January.
6. The concert is <u>on</u> August 24th.
7. They moved to Seoul <u>in</u> 2010.
8. I often go skiing <u>in</u> winter.
9. Bats hunt <u>at</u> night.

WRITING POINT ②

1. My uncle lives <u>in</u> Canada.
2. Please sit <u>on</u> the chair.
3. She is cooking <u>in</u> the kitchen.
4. She is standing <u>at</u> the bus stop.
5. They are resting <u>under</u> the tree.
6. A man sat <u>next to</u> me.
7. The parking lot is <u>behind</u> the building.
8. The bus stops <u>in front of</u> the hotel.
9. The table is <u>between</u> the beds.

SENTENCE PRACTICE 2
p.116

1. The play begins <u>at</u> 7:30.
2. My sister's wedding is <u>on</u> Friday.
3. We can see many different flowers <u>in</u> spring.
4. I always write a card to my mom <u>on her birthday</u>.
5. It is dangerous to walk alone <u>at</u> night.
6. They took a lot of photos <u>in</u> Europe.
7. There is someone <u>at</u> the door.
8. The man <u>next to</u> me kept talking loudly.

TRY WRITING
p.117

1. It often rains in July.
2. My parents got married in 2000.
3. There are two mosquitoes on the ceiling.
4. They are having dinner at the table.
5. She usually goes grocery shopping on Fridays.
6. The shop opens at 10 o'clock on Sunday morning.
7. A rabbit is hiding behind the bush.
8. Tim came back home at midnight yesterday.
9. The ship is passing under the bridge.
10. Susan is watering the flowers in the garden.
11. On the first day of school, I met a lot of new friends.
12. The moon is between the earth and the sun.

LESSON 24 접속사

CHECK UP
p.118

1. when
2. after
3. because
4. that
5. when
6. before
7. After
8. that
9. when
10. that

SENTENCE PRACTICE 1
p.119

WRITING POINT ①

1. <u>When</u> I arrive in London, I'll text you.
2. I feel good <u>when</u> I listen to music.
3. <u>Before</u> I go to bed, I read a book.
4. Jack exercises <u>before</u> he eats dinner.
5. <u>After</u> I wash my hair, I always dry it.
6. He got a job <u>after</u> he finished college.
7. I am hungry <u>because</u> I didn't eat lunch.
8. <u>Because</u> he was sick, he didn't go to work.

1. I think (that) Julie is pretty.

2. I believe (that) we will win the game.

3. I hope (that) it snows on Christmas day.

4. We know (that) John is honest.

5. I heard (that) you had a car accident.

6. He said (that) the movie was fantastic.

7. I thought (that) he was a student.

8. I didn't know (that) you liked Korean food.

9. I can't believe (that) he won the lottery.

SENTENCE PRACTICE 2 p.120

1. We stayed home all day because it rained a lot.

2. Can you close the window before you go out?

3. After he fell asleep, he had a strange dream.

4. My dog greets me when I get home.

5. When she heard the news, she jumped with joy.

6. I think that he has a good sense of humor.

7. I hope that you will get better soon.

8. We know that smoking is bad for our health.

9. People believe that a four-leaf clover brings them good luck.

10. Do you think that he is the best player on the team?

TRY WRITING p.121

1. Jack was late for school because he missed the bus.

2. I think (that) we have too much homework.

3. You should not[shouldn't] drive when you are tired.

4. They did not[didn't] go camping because it was too cold.

5. I drink hot tea when I have a cold.

6. I hope (that) you have a good time.

7. I believe (that) she will be a great pianist.

8. Jane and Bob bought popcorn before the movie started.

9. Do you think (that) there is life on Mars?

10. I always take a shower before I go to bed.

11. I cannot[can't] believe (that) we made it.

12. I did not[didn't] know (that) you won the first prize.

미리 보는 서술형 SCHOOL TEST p.122

1. (1) in   (2) at

2. July 10

3. ① at Busan → in Busan

   ③ on 6 a.m. → at 6 a.m.

   ⑤ in her birthday → on her birthday

4. (1) Two people are sitting on the bench.

   (2) The cat is sleeping behind the bag.

5. (1) between John and Mary

   (2) next to Lisa

   (3) in front of Lisa

6. (1) I think that he can pass the test.

   (2) I hope that we can see again.

7. (1) I learned to ride a bike when I was five.

   (2) Because it is raining, we can't play football.

UNIT 10

LESSON 25 명령문

CHECK UP p.124

1. Have   2. do   3. Be

4. Lend   5. turn   6. Don't

7. Don't be   8. leave   9. Don't

10. don't

SENTENCE PRACTICE 1 p.125

WRITING POINT ①

1. Close the window.

2. Take your umbrella.

3. Go to bed early.

4. Be confident.

5. Please pass me the salt.

6. Please come in and sit down.

7. <u>Do</u> your homework after school.

8. <u>Finish</u> your work before 6 o'clock.

WRITING POINT ❷

1. Don't <u>talk</u> too loudly.

2. Don't <u>fight</u> with your brother.

3. Don't <u>run</u> in the hallway.

4. Don't <u>play</u> the music.

5. Don't <u>be</u> shy.

6. Don't <u>listen</u> to him.

7. Don't <u>tell</u> lies to your parents.

8. Don't <u>be</u> afraid of making mistakes.

SENTENCE PRACTICE 2
p.126

1. <u>Put</u> the <u>milk</u> in the refrigerator.

2. <u>Stand</u> in line, <u>please</u>.

3. <u>Have</u> a <u>good</u> <u>time</u> with your family.

4. Always <u>be</u> <u>nice</u> to your sister.

5. <u>Please</u> <u>turn</u> <u>down</u> the music.

6. <u>Don't</u> <u>make</u> <u>noise</u> at night.

7. <u>Don't</u> <u>stay</u> in the sun too long.

8. <u>Don't</u> <u>be</u> <u>late</u> again.

9. <u>Don't</u> <u>forget</u> to bring your camera.

10. <u>Don't</u> <u>tell</u> <u>anybody</u> about it.

TRY WRITING
p.127

1. Turn right at the corner.

2. Don't jump on the bed.

3. Don't forget your cell phone.

4. Keep them in a safe place.

5. Take this medicine three times a day.

6. Don't watch too much TV.

7. Put the trash in the trash can.

8. Don't be rude to your teacher.

9. Don't cross the road at a red light.

10. Please be quiet during the presentation.

11. Don't play the piano late at night.

12. Put sunscreen before you go out.

LESSON 26 감탄문

CHECK UP
p.128

1. How

2. What

3. How

4. What

5. How

6. How

7. What

8. What

9. How

10. What

SENTENCE PRACTICE 1
p.129

WRITING POINT ❶

1. <u>What a big fish</u> it is!

2. <u>What a cheap bag</u> it is!

3. <u>What an interesting story</u> it is!

4. <u>What a good sister</u> you are!

5. <u>What good friends</u> they are!

6. <u>What a nice hat</u> you have!

7. <u>What a big house</u> he has!

8. <u>What a special day</u> it was!

9. <u>What a great job</u> he did!

WRITING POINT ❷

1. <u>How handsome</u> he is!

2. <u>How cold</u> it is!

3. <u>How sweet</u> this chocolate is!

4. <u>How brave</u> you are!

5. <u>How delicious</u> they are!

6. <u>How happy</u> she looks!

7. <u>How fast</u> he runs!

8. <u>How difficult</u> the test was!

9. <u>How beautiful</u> the sunset was!

SENTENCE PRACTICE 2
p.130

1. What <u>a</u> <u>great</u> <u>singer</u> <u>he</u> <u>is</u>!

2. What <u>good</u> <u>neighbors</u> <u>they</u> <u>are</u>!

3. What <u>a</u> <u>lovely</u> <u>smile</u> <u>she</u> <u>has</u>!

4. What <u>a</u> <u>nice</u> <u>shirt</u> <u>you</u> <u>are</u> <u>wearing</u>!

5. What <u>a</u> <u>long</u> <u>day</u> <u>it</u> <u>was</u>!

6. How <u>tired</u> <u>I</u> <u>am</u>!

7. How <u>busy</u> <u>you</u> <u>are</u>!

8. How <u>smart</u> <u>your</u> <u>dog</u> <u>is</u>!

9. How <u>slowly</u> <u>he</u> <u>speaks</u>!

10. How <u>beautifully</u> <u>she</u> <u>dances</u>!

1. How kind Mr. Kim is!
2. What a hot day it is!
3. How cheap the restaurant is!
4. How clean the streets are!
5. What a useful tip it is!
6. What a pretty bag you have!
7. How beautiful she looks!
8. What a great speech it was!
9. How wonderful the trip was!
10. What an exciting game it was!
11. How fast he is running!
12. What nice pictures you took!

LESSON 27 부가의문문

CHECK UP   p.132

1. aren't they   2. doesn't she   3. can't you
4. isn't he   5. didn't you   6. did they
7. wasn't she   8. were they   9. shouldn't I
10. does he

SENTENCE PRACTICE 1   p.133

WRITING POINT ❶

1. She is a good singer, isn't she?
2. You are my best friend, aren't you?
3. We are not late, are we?
4. They weren't at home, were they?
5. The movie was boring, wasn't it?

WRITING POINT ❷

1. She can speak English, can't she?
2. Tim can't drive a car, can he?
3. You won't go to the library, will you?
4. They will leave tomorrow, won't they?
5. I shouldn't buy the car, should I?

WRITING POINT ❸

1. You have a brother, don't you?
2. He teaches English, doesn't he?
3. They don't know each other, do they?
4. You lived near here, didn't you?
5. They didn't have lunch, did they?

SENTENCE PRACTICE 2   p.134

1. You are not ready yet, are you?
2. They are from London, aren't they?
3. Her hair wasn't long, was it?
4. They can't catch the train, can they?
5. You will invite him to dinner, won't you?
6. We should start now, shouldn't we?
7. You don't like spicy food, do you?
8. The supermarket closes at midnight, doesn't it?
9. The pants don't fit you, do they?
10. They went to the theater last night, didn't they?

TRY WRITING ✎   p.135

1. You are not[aren't] tired, are you?
2. She has two children, doesn't she?
3. You cannot[can't] speak French, can you?
4. This shirt is too big for me, isn't it?
5. You live in a big city, don't you?
6. Mr. Lee was your homeroom teacher, wasn't he?
7. You will not[won't] tell the secret, will you?
8. They did not[didn't] win the game, did they?
9. She doesn't drink coffee, does she?
10. The glasses are yours, aren't they?
11. Jack, you borrowed my book, didn't you?
12. You will take care of the dog, won't you?

미리 보는 서술형 SCHOOL TEST   p.136

1. (1) Turn   (2) Don't run   (3) Don't be
2. (1) Be quite   (2) Don't take the books
   (3) Return books
3. How tall this building is
4. (1) kind you are
   (2) beautiful flowers they are
5. does he
6. (1) is it   (2) can't you
   (3) didn't he
7. (1) This book is interesting, isn't it?
   (2) You didn't lock the door, did you?

WORKBOOK

LESSON 01 동사와 인칭대명사

p.003

1. She is a middle school student.
2. It is in my bag.
3. You are good neighbors.
4. They are sisters.
5. We are at the airport.
6. Tom and I are in the same class.
7. I am tired and sleepy.
8. My birthday is in April.
9. Rick and I are close friends.
10. These pants are too big for me.
11. She is polite to people.
12. My favorite season is summer.
13. My brother is good at sports.
14. The café is on the second floor.
15. They are on vacation in Hawaii.

LESSON 02 be동사의 부정문, 의문문

p.005

1. I am not a good cook.
2. She is not in her room.
3. This soup is not warm.
4. Those shoes are not mine.
5. Is he a famous writer?
6. Are they in the living room?
7. I am not a liar.
8. The weather is not cold today.
9. Are you interested in music?
10. Are your parents strict?
11. Are we ready to go?
12. These vegetables are not fresh.
13. We are not in class right now.
14. Are Mina and Minji twins?
15. Are you afraid of dogs?

LESSON 03 일반동사의 긍정문

p.007

1. I eat breakfast every day.
2. They watch TV in the evening.
3. The students wear school uniforms.
4. She practices the violin every day.
5. He goes to school by bus.
6. She teaches English at school.
7. My sister has curly hair.
8. We enjoy outdoor sports on weekends.
9. Greg and Kelly study in the library after school.
10. Many foreigners learn Korean these days.
11. He usually eats sandwiches for lunch.
12. Minsu reads comic books in his free time.
13. Cathy washes her hair every morning.
14. He walks his dog every day.
15. The birds fly very high.

LESSON 04 일반동사의 부정문, 의문문

p.009

1. I don't study at night.
2. She doesn't drink coffee.
3. The bus doesn't stop here.
4. Do you like Chinese food?
5. Does he play the drums?
6. Do they work on Saturday?
7. Does your father often cook?
8. It doesn't snow in Australia.
9. We don't have much time.
10. The restaurant doesn't serve breakfast.
11. I don't like hot weather.
12. The computer doesn't work well.
13. Does this bus go to the airport?
14. John doesn't have many friends at school.
15. Do people in your country use chopsticks?

LESSON 05 be동사의 과거형

p.011

1. I was sick yesterday.
2. My mother was a nurse.
3. We were late for school this morning.

4. He wasn't in London in 2010.

5. They weren't tired.

6. Were you at home last weekend?

7. Was the hotel comfortable?

8. My sister was born in May.

9. Frankfurt was the capital of Germany.

10. They weren't close to each other.

11. The umbrella wasn't in the car.

12. Was the movie good last night?

13. The book was under my bed.

14. It was my mistake.

15. My parents and I were on vacation last week.

LESSON 06 일반동사의 과거형

p.013

1. We went home early.

2. He passed the exam.

3. She didn't eat the food.

4. We didn't hear the news.

5. Did you find your key?

6. Did they win the game?

7. We went to the movies last Friday.

8. Mr. Brown invited us to dinner.

9. I left my bag on the bus.

10. They didn't come to my birthday party.

11. Did I make a mistake?

12. Did they enjoy their holiday?

13. The train didn't arrive on time.

14. Lisa cut her finger in art class.

15. Steve didn't sleep well last night.

LESSON 07 현재진행형

p.015

1. They are walking along the beach.

2. The girl is sitting on the bench.

3. You aren't wearing glasses.

4. Are you listening to me?

5. Are Kevin and Lisa doing their homework?

6. The children are crossing the street.

7. The guests are taking off their coats.

8. You aren't telling me the truth.

9. Are they talking on the phone now?

10. She is drinking a cup of tea.

11. You are singing too loudly.

12. Is he using the copy machine?

13. Are you looking for your car keys?

14. My grandmother is watering the flowers in the garden.

15. Are Tom and Rachael waiting for the school bus?

LESSON 08 will, be going to

p.017

1. Eric will drive us to the station.

2. I will not take a bus. I will walk.

3. Some people will not believe this.

4. Will you be at home this evening?

5. I am going to move into a new house next month.

6. He is going to leave for Busan tomorrow.

7. Are they going to work this Saturday?

8. I will do my best.

9. They are going to get married next month.

10. Will you be a movie director in the future?

11. His son will be fifteen years old next month.

12. You will not have any problems.

13. Ted is going to fly to London in July.

14. I will be ready in five minutes.

15. In the future, people will travel to other planets.

LESSON 09 can, may

p.019

1. I can play the violin.

2. He may be sick today.

3. May I ask a question?

4. We cannot[can't] live without water.

5. Can you help me with my homework?

6. Tom can swim and play table tennis very well.

7. It may snow next week.

8. She may not like seafood.

9. You may/can use the computers in the library.

10. May/Can I try on these shoes?

11. Some people can speak three languages.

12. My grandfather cannot[can't] read without glasses.
13. I cannot[can't] find my key anywhere.
14. He can run 100 meters in 12 seconds.
15. Your purse may be on the table.

LESSON 10 must, have to, should

p.021

1. You must answer all the questions.
2. Students must hand in their homework by tomorrow.
3. Jane must not eat too much junk food.
4. He has to get up early tomorrow morning.
5. You don't have to say sorry.
6. You should exercise regularly.
7. He should not stay up too late.
8. Jake should spend more time with his family.
9. You must keep your promise.
10. I have to finish my homework today.
11. People must not smoke in public places.
12. You don't have to worry about it.
13. They should not buy the house.
14. You must not use your cell phone during the class.
15. They don't have to pay for dinner.

LESSON 11 when, where

p.023

1. When is Jane's birthday?
2. Where are you from?
3. When does he practice tennis?
4. Where do you buy your clothes?
5. When did she call you?
6. Where did he leave his umbrella?
7. Where were you after school?
8. When does the movie start?
9. When does the next bus arrive?
10. When did you lose your sunglasses?
11. Where do koalas live?
12. Where is the nearest bus stop?
13. When did you travel to Japan?
14. When did the accident happen?
15. Where was the missing child?

LESSON 12 who, what

p.025

1. What color is his car?
2. Who do you work with?
3. What is in the box?
4. What happened to him?
5. Who did he invite to the party?
6. What does this word mean?
7. What time do you usually go to bed?
8. Who is sitting on the sofa?
9. Who stole his wallet yesterday?
10. Who is in the kitchen?
11. What was your biggest mistake?
12. Who turned off the alarm?
13. What do you usually do in your free time?
14. Who do you respect the most?
15. What do you want for your birthday?

LESSON 13 why, how

p.027

1. Why is she so happy?
2. Why are the children laughing?
3. How was your Christmas?
4. How did they meet each other?
5. Why was he late for the meeting?
6. How was your trip to Spain?
7. How does this machine work?
8. How often do you visit your grandparents?
9. How many times do you eat out a month?
10. How far is your school from here?
11. How is the weather in your country?
12. How was your math test?
13. How do you spell your name?
14. Why are you in a hurry?
15. How many tickets do you need?

LESSON 14 There is/are, 비인칭 주어 it

p.029

1. It is my birthday today.
2. What time is it now?
3. What day is it today?
4. There is a big tree in the garden.

5. There are thirty students in our class.

6. There isn't any water in the glass.

7. Is there a parking lot near here?

8. How many people are there in your family?

9. It is very hot in here.

10. Is it raining outside?

11. It was warm and sunny yesterday.

12. There are four seasons in a year.

13. There aren't many flowers in the garden.

14. There is a concert in the park this evening.

15. It takes 10 minutes by bike.

LESSON 15 감각동사+형용사

p.031

1. You look tired today.

2. Her voice sounds beautiful.

3. The vegetables don't look fresh.

4. Does it taste good?

5. This picture looks like a photo.

6. It sounds like a good plan.

7. What does he look like?

8. This medicine tastes bitter.

9. This sofa feels comfortable.

10. This shampoo smells like roses.

11. This ice cream tastes like green tea.

12. His explanation sounds difficult.

13. I feel lonely without you.

14. I sometimes feel like a genius.

15. Dave felt nervous before the speech.

LESSON 16 수여동사

p.033

1. I wrote Mike an email.

2. He showed me a picture.

3. Mr. Kim teaches us math.

4. He made us pizza.

5. He asked me a question.

6. I bought a toy car for my brother.

7. They always tell the truth to each other.

8. Frank told us a funny story.

9. The trip gave me a special experience.

10. My uncle sent me a present on my birthday.

11. My dad cooks us dinner once a week.

12. Linda made a nice hat for me.

13. Mike doesn't lend his car to anyone.

14. Mindy taught some Chinese characters to me.

15. He bought a puppy for his daughter.

LESSON 17 to부정사의 명사적 용법

p.035

1. It is useful to learn a foreign language.

2. It is fun to go camping.

3. My hobby is to read novels.

4. I want to travel around the world.

5. It is never boring to live in Seoul.

6. It is healthy to eat vegetables.

7. His dream is to be president.

8. Jim and Sue want to spend time together.

9. Mary likes to take pictures.

10. Why did you decide to be a singer?

11. It is not easy to get up at 6 in the morning.

12. My homework is to write about my special talent.

13. It is impossible to finish the work by tomorrow.

14. We plan to visit the nursing home this weekend.

15. It was very easy to solve the math problem.

LESSON 18 to부정사의 형용사적, 부사적 용법

p.037

1. You need a jacket to wear at night.

2. He has many friends to help him.

3. There are many places to visit in Korea.

4. People exercise to stay healthy.

5. I went to the library to study.

6. He turned on the radio to listen to music.

7. Everyone needs someone to love.

8. I have a lot of homework to do this week.

9. They are looking for a house to live in.

10. He goes jogging every morning to lose weight.

11. I went to the park to walk my dog.

12. It is time to have lunch.

13. He introduced a way to reduce air pollution.

14. Minsu studied all night to get good grades.

15. Do you have a pen to write with?

LESSON 19 동명사

p.039

1. Driving in the rain is dangerous.
2. Being/Staying at home all day is boring.
3. Exercising every day is not easy.
4. Drinking enough water is good for you.
5. My favorite thing is playing basketball.
6. I enjoy watching movies.
7. They finished doing their homework.
8. Giving up easily is a bad habit.
9. Building a house takes a lot of time.
10. His secret to success is always doing his best.
11. Her job is helping sick people.
12. I sometimes enjoy being alone.
13. They kept talking during the class.
14. My goal is getting a good score in math.
15. You should avoid eating too much junk food.

LESSON 20 수량 형용사, 빈도부사

p.041

1. Are there many books in the library?
2. He doesn't drink much coffee.
3. They asked a lot of questions.
4. We bought a lot of food.
5. I usually walk to school.
6. Do you often exercise?
7. I will never see him again.
8. We have a lot of problems to solve.
9. It is often cloudy in London.
10. You should not eat too many sweets.
11. We don't have much time to finish the work.
12. I met a lot of foreigners at the festival.
13. My father is always busy at work.
14. She spends too much money on clothes.
15. You can always ask me for help.

LESSON 21 비교급, 최상급

p.043

1. My bag is heavier than yours.
2. For me, English is easier than math.
3. Sally is the youngest of the three.
4. The Nile is the longest river in the world.
5. Sharks are the most dangerous animals in the sea.
6. Mangos are sweeter than oranges.
7. Snow White is more beautiful than the witch.
8. There are more girls than boys in the class.
9. Today is the happiest day in my life.
10. This is the cheapest restaurant in the town.
11. He is the fastest runner in the world.
12. Turtles live longer than other animals.
13. What is the highest mountain in the world?
14. Ice hockey is the most popular sport in Canada.
15. What is the most important thing in your life?

LESSON 22 원급 비교

p.045

1. This bed is as hard as a rock.
2. Her skin is as white as snow.
3. The water is as cold as ice.
4. Jane plays tennis as well as Jim.
5. My hair is not as long as yours.
6. The moon is not as bright as the sun.
7. This summer is not as hot as last summer.
8. His idea is not as good as yours.
9. John works as hard as Mark.
10. Bill is as tall as his father.
11. This new sofa is as comfortable as the old one.
12. Money is not as important as good health.
13. I can jump as high as you.
14. He is running as fast as he can.
15. I do not watch TV as much as you.

p.047

1. We have lunch at noon.
2. The concert is on August 24th.
3. They moved to Seoul in 2010.
4. She is standing at the bus stop.
5. A man sat next to me.
6. It is dangerous to walk alone at night.
7. I saw your laptop on the sofa in the living room.
8. Let's meet in front of the theater at 5:30.
9. It often rains in July.
10. There are two mosquitoes on the ceiling.
11. She usually goes grocery shopping on Fridays.
12. The shop opens at 10 o'clock on Sunday morning.
13. A rabbit is hiding behind the bush.
14. The ship is passing under the bridge.
15. The moon is between the earth and the sun.

p.049

1. When I arrive in London, I'll text you.
2. He got a job after he finished college.
3. I hope that it snows on Christmas day.
4. I cannot[can't] believe that he won the lottery.
5. Can you close the window before you go out?
6. After he fell asleep, he had a strange dream.
7. When she heard the news, she jumped with joy.
8. I think that he has a good sense of humor.
9. We know that smoking is bad for our health.
10. People believe that a four-leaf clover brings them good luck.
11. Jack was late for school because he missed the bus.
12. I drink hot tea when I have a cold.
13. Do you think that there is life on Mars?
14. I cannot[can't] believe that we made it.
15. I didn't know that you won the first prize.

p.051

1. Be kind to other people.
2. Please pass me the salt.
3. Don't fight with your brother.
4. Don't run in the hallway.
5. Put the milk in the refrigerator.
6. Stand in line, please.
7. Please turn down the music.
8. Don't make noise at night.
9. Don't be late again.
10. Don't forget to bring your camera.
11. Turn right at the corner.
12. Keep them in a safe place.
13. Take this medicine three times a day.
14. Put the trash in the trash can.
15. Don't be rude to your teacher.

p.053

1. What an interesting book it is!
2. What a great job he did!
3. How big the watermelon is!
4. How cold it is!
5. How brave you are!
6. How happy she looks!
7. What good neighbors they are!
8. What a lovely smile she has!
9. What a nice shirt you are wearing!
10. What a long day it was!
11. How tired I am!
12. How beautifully she dances!
13. What an exciting game it was!
14. How fast he is running!
15. What nice pictures you took!

p.055

1. The garden is beautiful, isn't it?
2. You are my best friend, aren't you?
3. The movie was boring, wasn't it?
4. She can speak English, can't she?

5. They will leave tomorrow, won't they?
6. I shouldn't buy the car, should I?
7. They don't know each other, do they?
8. You will invite him to dinner, won't you?
9. You don't like spicy food, do you?
10. The supermarket closes at midnight, doesn't it?
11. They went to the theater last night, didn't they?
12. This shirt is too big for me, isn't it?
13. You live in a big city, don't you?
14. The glasses are yours, aren't they?
15. Jack, you borrowed my book, didn't you?

MEMO

MEMO